THE GREAT CRASH OF 2008

THE
GREAT
CRASH
OF
2008

ROSS GARNAUT

with

DAVID LLEWELLYN-SMITH

MELBOURNE
UNIVERSITY
PRESS

MELBOURNE UNIVERSITY PRESS
An imprint of Melbourne University Publishing Limited
187 Grattan Street, Carlton, Victoria 3053, Australia
mup-info@unimelb.edu.au
www.mup.com.au

First published 2009
Text © Ross Garnaut, David Llewellyn-Smith 2009
Design and typography © Melbourne University Publishing Limited, 2009

Designed by Nada Backovic
Typeset by Megan Ellis
Cover design by Design by Committee
Printed by Griffin Press, South Australia

National Library of Australia Cataloguing-in-Publication entry:

Garnaut, Ross.

The great crash of 2008/Ross Garnaut with David Llewellyn-Smith.

9780522857023 (pbk.)

Includes index.

Financial crises—History—21st century.
Financial crises—United States.
Business cycles—History—21st century.
Recessions—History—21st century
Credit—United States.
Climatic changes—Economic aspects.
United States—Economic policy.
United States—Economic conditions—21st century.

Llewellyn Smith, David.

330.9

CONTENTS

Preface

On the morning of 30 September 2008 I handed the
Garnaut Climate Change Review to the Prime Minister
of Australia, Kevin Rudd. The review had absorbed the
majority of my waking hours—and quite a few more—
for eighteen months.

The Prime Minister at first mainly wanted to talk
about a cataclysm in financial markets. Overnight—that
morning Australian time—the New York Stock Exchange
had suffered its largest ever points fall in a single day and
all of the media talk was of collapse of the international
financial system and of imminent global recession.
Certainly when it was time for us to meet members of
the media, the financial crisis was in the forefront of their
minds.

In other times, I would have closely followed the
unravelling of global finance as it was happening, as
international money is one of my oldest and closest
professional interests. In 1998 Ross McLeod and I had
published the first book on the Asian financial crisis,

but this new crisis had crept up while I was submerged in my preoccupation with a diabolical long-term policy problem.

I had a lot of catching up to do. After three months' intensive discussion of the climate change review, I began reading the serious things that had been written about the financial crisis. Melbourne University Publishing's Louise Adler came across me at this time and said that the subject needed a book that pulled it all together. Glyn Davis, the university's vice-chancellor, added his weight to the call.

So then I had to write it, quickly and in an unconscionably busy life. Fortunately David Llewellyn-Smith had just created some room in his own professional life by selling *The Diplomat*, the international affairs magazine that he had founded and run through a successful decade. David had followed international finance in the magazine, and was assiduously following the news through the blogs and other channels. We found ourselves in long conversations about the clever money that was coming undone. Here was rich complementarity!

The rest, as they say, is history. The publisher kept reminding us that readers were anxiously waiting for the answers to their questions. And here they are, six months after the book's conception.

Ross Garnaut
University of Melbourne
August 2009

Acknowledgements

Like the cave paintings of Dunhuang, the thoughts that are captured in a book have been partially formed in many minds, and transmitted backwards and forwards by voice or script through many channels before taking their final shape. Ross's thoughts on these issues have been formed over many decades through interaction with old and current colleagues at the Australian National University and the University of Melbourne. David's were strongly influenced by the productive interaction with many contributors to *The Diplomat*, and many other interlocutors during those years and since.

We would like to acknowledge the special assistance of a number of people for insights and for gathering the material that is the empirical flesh of the book: Philip Bayley, Andrew Boughton, Kym Dalton, Matthew Hardman, John Hampton, David James, Brian Johnson, Alister Maitland, Graham O'Neil, Ian Rogers, Bernard Salt, Christopher Selth and Grant Turner. Sui Lay, a graduate student at the Melbourne Institute, University of Melbourne, gave us valuable assistance with data. We thank Veronica Webster for library research and other support.

We are grateful to colleagues and other friends who discussed ideas at length or commented on drafts, including, Max Corden, Andrew Charlton, Peter Drysdale, John Garnaut, Jill and Michael Lester, Justin Lin, Sri Mulyani, Steve Sedgewick, and participants in the seminar at the Melbourne Institute of Applied Economic and Social Research at the University of Melbourne.

Ross thanks Jayne for sharing it all again. David thanks Belinda for her support and endurance through author's widowhood.

Ross Garnaut
David Llewellyn-Smith

Introduction

Many articles and books have already been written in search of the cause of the Great Crash of 2008. In reading these, we are reminded of the old Indian story of the blind men seeking to describe an elephant. One blind man feels the trunk and says that an elephant is like a snake. One feels the tail and disputes the serpentine explanation. 'No,' he says, 'an elephant is like a rope'. One puts his arm around a leg and likens an elephant to a tree. One feels a large ear and says that an elephant is like a fan.

A phenomenon as complex, large and damaging as the Great Crash of 2008 has many parts. This book seeks to describe the whole elephant.

There are Boom and Panic explanations for the crisis. Financial euphorias and crises have ended in recession and depression since the emergence of capitalism in Western Europe in the seventeenth century. Some economists have noted the increasing frequency and severity of major financial crises in recent decades. For them, the Great

Crash of 2008 followed a great boom in a way that is familiar from history.[1]

To this we can add the more recent views of the behavioural economists. They observe that humans are not always the rational, calculating beings familiar from economic texts. Individuals tend to run with the herd, behaviour that was hard-wired from human experience long before the origins of the modern market economy. The herd behaviour exaggerates the booms and also the panics, as well as the contractions that follow.[2]

There are Global Imbalances explanations for the crisis. At first the imbalances were principally between English-speaking (Anglosphere)[3] deficit nations and Asia's export-oriented surplus economies. As the boom reached fever pitch from 2004, commodity prices rose and rose. Huge surpluses appeared in commodity-exporting countries, especially oil producers.[4] Old economics says that such large imbalances end in tears, especially for the deficit countries. We saw it in the lead-up to depressions in the 1890s and the 1930s. Something would happen to make it hard to fund the deficits, and this would force a huge contraction. In the modern era of floating exchange rates, many economists said that imbalances didn't matter anymore. The Global Imbalances theorists say they do, and were an important cause of the Crash.

There are Clever Money explanations for the crisis. These propose that the modern world of complex finance and its many new financial instruments, all managed on an incomprehensible scale, were an accident waiting to happen. Astute observers of the financial markets argue that the people introducing Clever Money neither understood, nor wanted to understand, its risks.[5] The new financial instruments contained risks that were bound to lead to a collapse.

There has also been considerable discussion of the role of Greed in the Crash. Reduced moral standards in financial markets and weakened constraints on private enrichment created risks for others. This explanation has been emphasised as a causal factor by new Christian Social Democratic leaders in the Anglosphere, notably Barack Obama in the United States and Kevin Rudd in Australia. These leaders came to office after the first whiff of rotten finance wafted from markets in early 2007.[6]

Booms and Panics, Global Imbalances, Clever Money and Greed are all part of the story of the Great Crash of 2008. The elephant takes its form from the way in which these four parts fit together.

The Anglosphere asset booms that preceded the Crash were encouraged by a long period of historically low interest rates in the 1990s and even lower beyond the millennium. Fiscal and tax policies, demographic shifts and migration exaggerated the boom. The illusion of wealth created by the asset booms drove a huge consumption binge. This was part of the story of the large growth in imports from Asian developing countries that specialised in exports of low-cost manufactured goods. Over time, as Anglosphere nations spent more than they earned, they developed large balance of payments deficits. These were matched by equally large surpluses elsewhere, especially in the export-oriented developing economies. These surpluses were then lent back to the Anglosphere, further extending asset inflation and completing what seemed a virtuous cycle.

Funding the dearth of savings in the Anglosphere became an important part of business for the North Atlantic banks that dominated global finance. The payment imbalances and the banks that transferred the funds grew together. The banks and other financial firms invented ever more creative ways to lure the surplus savings into Anglosphere mortgages and business loans. These arcane arts of Clever Money were motivated by new incentive structures that delivered enormous incomes to those who could demonstrate large short-term earnings. The future was heavily discounted. Greed, that old ally of every boom, helped to push the boundaries of financial innovation and government regulation. A brave new world of financial risk emerged.

The Crash of September and October 2008 was followed immediately by the Great Recession. Global output, incomes and trade in the time from the Great Crash to this book going to press in July 2009 have fallen more than in the corresponding early stages of the Great Depression, which followed the Great Crash of 1929. Governments have responded with much greater reductions of interest rates and loosening of budgets than occurred post-1929.

To understand the causes and effects of the Great Crash, it is necessary to grasp that a fundamental economic change was underway that raised global living standards in sustainable ways. We call this period of rapidly rising incomes for many of the world's people the Platinum Age. It was centred in the large developing countries, most importantly China and then India. These countries opened themselves up to the global economy in the late twentieth century. Their subsequent growth raised incomes, savings and investment in the world as a whole. This justified some increase in global asset prices. However, the market response to this growth extended the asset booms beyond all reason. *without reason*

In the best of circumstances, the legacy of the Great Crash in the major developed countries that were running large payments deficits, and which had serious flaws in their financial systems, will be long, costly and painful. On the other hand, there are early signs that there may be relatively little disruption of Platinum Age growth in *why* China and some other major developing countries. The *the Great* surplus developing countries are in a strong position to *Crash* stimulate internal demand and switch to growth that is *had little* much less reliant on external demand. *effect on China*

One consequence of the divergent fortunes of the large developing countries and of the deficit economies of the developed world will be the acceleration of a shift in the global economic and geostrategic balance. Managing this premature shift will complicate the response to the great challenges facing the international community, including the mitigation of human-induced global warming, the alleviation of poverty in the many poor developing countries that have been damaged severely by the Great Recession, and the management of the trade and financial problems that have arisen in or been exacerbated by the Great Crash.

The Great Crash of 2008 and the subsequent Great Recession are creating significant ideological and policy legacies. The elephant is reshaping the world.

Part I
Boom

1

The Platinum Age

IN 1986 AN AUSTRALIAN delegation met the diminu-^{small}
tive Chinese leader, Deng Xiaoping. As the little great
man aimed a projectile into his spittoon, the Australian
ambassador successfully resisted an impulse to withdraw his adjacent shoe. He had just asked Deng what
he had meant when he said that his long-term ambition
was for China to enjoy the living standards of middle-
income industrialising countries by 2050. Did he mean
the incomes of people in economies such as Taiwan
and the Republic of Korea at that time, or the expected
incomes of the mid twenty-first century?

Deng finished clearing his chain-smoking throat and
replied: 'The average of those middle-income economies
now. Then I hope that the Chinese people will be
satisfied'.

By 2009 the output per head of the Chinese on the mainland had reached the level that Deng had hoped for. But being an ungrateful lot, there is no sign of the satiation of their desire for material progress. Whatever this great twentieth-century leader may have wished for them, the Chinese people have made it clear that they will not happily settle for less than Americans, Japanese or Europeans. And the experience of another quarter-century of reform and growth has made it clear that they probably won't have to.

The early twenty-first century brought the most widely based and rapid sustained economic growth that the world has ever known. Its essence was the extension of the beneficent processes of modern economic growth to the vast interiors of the populous countries of Asia. China led the way and was followed by Indonesia, India and others. More people were elevated from poverty than ever before over a comparably short period. We call this period the Platinum Age.[1]

The strong sustained growth of the large developing countries is transforming the global economy and its geostrategic context. It is fundamentally changing the way in which people look at their history and their prospects. Yet it is a natural phenomenon, growing from roots established in much smaller societies more than 200 years ago, and evolving over the years since. These powerful historical processes now have their centre in East Asia, and yet there is no East Asian miracle. What is at work is the extension into new places of well-established, well-understood economics.

Sustained, rapid economic growth is now the process by which a poor and economically backward country catches up with the technology, business organisation and capital intensity of the advanced economies. The 'catching up' happens naturally when certain conditions are met. The central precondition is that there is an effective state, able to offer stability in political and economic institutions, and to enforce the legal basis of market exchange.

Within a framework of political stability, the society has to accept the priority of the economic growth objective. [water] move around

Rapid economic growth is disruptive. It churns and reorders elites. It challenges the myths and institutions that give meaning to many people's lives. All of these tendencies generate reaction and resistance. But governments persist with policies that underpin rapid growth if the reasons for doing so are powerful enough to overcome the resistance.

Such growth requires a relatively high rate of investment, including in education. A high investment rate, if it is to be sustained during years that can be smooth or rough for the international economy, in turn needs to be built on a relatively high domestic savings rate. This is not so demanding a condition as it once seemed. There are now many cases of rapid economic growth in what had been a poor developing country being associated with significant increases in the savings rate. This has been evident in China throughout the reform period since 1978, and has recently been powerfully evident in India.

The education requirement becomes more demanding as successful economic development raises the technological complexity of the economy.

Sustained, rapid economic growth also requires the acceptance of a considerable role for markets in domestic and international exchange. It is necessary to get rid of the extremes of protection against imports that have been present in almost all developing countries.

For the first century and a half after the beginnings of modern capitalist development, contemporary economic growth was mostly confined to Western Europe and its overseas offshoots in North America and Oceania. The one major exception was Japan, which, after early rejection of the new ideas and technologies of the West, changed dramatically in the 1860s. Japanese elites realised that Japan's autonomy and sovereignty would be undermined by a commitment to the old ways.[2]

A huge gap emerged between the productivity and economic and military weight of the countries that had accepted the new ways of economic organisation, and those that had not. This became the basis of modern colonialism, through which a small proportion of the world's people ruled vast numbers far and wide. Colonialism mostly retarded the establishment of the essential conditions for sustained, rapid economic growth among the colonised peoples with histories of an effective state.

The first new participants in this growth, after Japan in the nineteenth century, emerged in the third quarter of the twentieth century. All were relatively small economies in East Asia: Hong Kong, Taiwan, South Korea and Singapore. Their success encouraged emulation by neighbours, and by the 1970s they had been joined by Thailand and Malaysia. The success of internationally oriented growth policies in relatively small East Asian developing economies was influential in the region's more populous countries. China moved decisively to a new development strategy when the senior revolutionary general and victim of the Cultural Revolution, Deng Xiaoping, received majority support in the Communist Party's Central Committee in December 1978.

Deng and his supporters had no blueprint for a new economic policy. In this they were like the leaders of Taiwan and South Korea in the first two decades after World War II, or Japan at the time of the Meiji Restoration. What was common in the early stages of all of these success stories was a commitment to the greater use of markets in domestic exchange, to international orientation, to making foreign trade a normal part of economic activity, and to absorbing successful technology, business organisation and capital from abroad.

China's progress has been inexorable, *unstoppable* except for two years around the political traumas of 1989–90 when the reforms were seriously challenged within the political elite. In the first thirty years of the reform era, real output grew at an average of 9.8 per cent per annum, real exports by 12.5 per cent and real imports by 11.7 per cent. The investment share of GDP rose from 29 per cent in the eighties to 38 per cent in 2008. The savings share over the same period rose from 29 per cent to 48 per cent.[3]

Ideas and technology from abroad were absorbed through students studying overseas, the purchase of technology and, over the past decade, increasingly through direct foreign investment and the internet. Direct foreign investment in China has represented a significant part of capital formation from the early 1990s, reaching an average of $80 billion per annum in the early twenty-first century, in some years the largest in the world, and around half of all such investment in developing countries.[4]

Indonesia, the world's fourth most populous country, committed itself unambiguously to deeper integration into the international economy in a series of steps from the mid 1960s, but most decisively in the decade from the mid 1980s. It was followed by the Philippines and Vietnam in the early 1990s, making the South-East Asian countries a substantial and rapidly growing part of the world economy. India committed itself to internationally oriented growth policies from 1991. Its growth in output and foreign trade, and its use of direct foreign investment, has accelerated steadily since then.[5]

The South-East Asian economies and South Korea suffered a major setback in a financial panic that precipitated deep recession in 1997–98.[6] This was the first major financial crisis of the era of globalisation. It had its origins in the private sector, rather than in the government budget deficits that had caused many earlier troubles in developing countries. The crisis emerged from the interaction between two weaknesses. One concerned flaws in financial institutions and in financial regulation. The other was corruption and cronyism in relations between government and business. In these and other ways, it was the precursor to the global Great Crash of 2008.

By the early twenty-first century, two decades of sustained economic growth had made China a substantial player in the world economy. It became so big that rapid growth in its output, demand and trade raised the world's rate of growth. In 2001, China became a member of the World Trade Organization, making stronger promises to open its economy to foreign trade than any other country had made on entry to the group. Even faster growth followed in China's trade: from 2001 to 2008, the country's output, exports and imports increased at average rates of 10.2, 20.8 and 18.6 per cent per annum respectively. China's share of world output measured in purchasing power rose from 1.8 per cent in 1980 to 11.4 per cent in 2008. Its share of world exports rose from 1.6 to 11 per cent, while its share of world imports grew from 1.4 to 8.3 per cent. China's exports grew at nearly five times the rate of growth of the world total and imports at almost four times the world total in the first eight years of the new millennium.

This strong growth in China, India and other large developing countries created trade opportunities for others. Japan's long stagnation, for example, was broken by large increases in exports to China. Growth in demand in these countries pushed most metals and energy prices to unprecedented levels, and boosted incomes and opportunities for profitable investment in commodity exporting countries. Exceptional global prosperity followed. Increased specialisation across countries in all economic activities, and greater international trade and investment, raised productivity and incomes almost everywhere.

2

The Greatest Bubble
in History

IN 1997 A LOW-BUDGET Australian movie dominated the national box office. *The Castle* cost $500 000 and took nineteen days to shoot. The movie's title was drawn from the platitude 'Each man's home is his castle'. Its major theme was an examination of the rights and value pertaining to home ownership.

The lead character, Darryl Kerrigan, was an iconic figure of Australiana: working-class, egalitarian and down-to-earth, someone who might have been described as a 'good bloke'. He was played by the lanky, laconic Michael Caton, whose moustachioed credulity encapsulated Australia's most adored self-image. The film held an ironic mirror up to Australia. On display were those dimensions of the nation that did not fit with its self-image of giving everyone a 'fair go'.

The Castle's launch coincided with changes that curtailed the realisation of traditional, passionately held goals of home ownership. That great Australian (or American or British) dream was mutating into volatile and dynamic asset trading. There is no better symbol for this shift than the subsequent career of Michael Caton. After the success of *The Castle*, he was recruited to host a major television series called *Hot Property*. In a case of life ignoring art, the man behind Darryl Kerrigan, the embodiment of passionate owner-occupation, became the face of asset speculation. The program offered tips on how to buy, renovate and sell property. This theme grew so strong with passing seasons that in 2000 it was renamed *Hot Auctions*. This was the very opposite of the quaint owner-occupier culture venerated in *The Castle*.

What drove this transformation?

Anglosphere house prices had boomed before. They had surged in the late 1980s as corporate freewheeling stoked growth within economies that had experienced recent financial liberalisation. However, the rise in prices was soon brought to heal by high interest rates and then the early 1990s recession.

But the boom that emerged in the mid 1990s went much further. It was described by *The Economist* in 2005 as the 'greatest bubble in history':

Never before have real house prices risen so fast, for so long, in so many countries. Property markets have been frothing from America, Britain and Australia to France, Spain and China. Rising property prices helped to prop up the world economy after the stockmarket bubble burst

in 2000. What if the housing boom now turns
to bust?[1]

The Economist estimated that from 2000 to 2005,
global housing more than doubled in value to more than
$70 trillion.

The Great Moderation

The story of the great Anglosphere asset bubble begins
with an atypical period of economic calm. Western
economists and officials began to note in the late 1990s
that volatility in their economies was in decline. By
this they meant that the frequency and depth of swings
between periods of growth and recession had diminished.
Inflation was under control and there was less need to
raise interest rates to high levels.

This phenomenon was called The Great Moderation
by the economist James Stock of the Kennedy School of
Government, Harvard University.[2] The term caught on.
Central banks around the world claimed that The Great
Moderation was the result of their increasingly compe-
tent use of interest rate policy. However, Stock attributed
the decline in volatility as much to the good luck of living
through a period with limited external shocks, such as
commodity price spikes induced by supply disruptions.

Other explanations for The Great Moderation have
included the mitigating effects of information technology
on the inventory cycle; the anxieties and competitive
pressures of globalisation deterring labour unions'
pursuit of higher wages; the increased role of services

in the economy and the corresponding reduction in the potency of the 'stock cycle'; and the disinflationary effects of expanding exports from China and other developing countries with low labour costs.

Whatever the mix of forces that produced subdued consumer price inflation through the early 1990s, the calm enabled a new set of central bank practices to emerge.

Liberated by the apparent defeat of inflation, the United States Federal Reserve under Alan Greenspan adopted a 'risk management' approach to monetary policy during crises. Greenspan, who had been appointed chairman of the Board of Governors in 1987 and held the post for a record period of almost twenty years, repeatedly shifted US interest rates lower in response to financial and other shocks. He did so following the 1987 stock market crash, the first Gulf War, the Mexican debt crisis, the Asian Financial Crisis, the Long Term Capital Management crisis, Y2K, the 'tech wreck' stock market crash and the September 11 terrorist attacks. No matter what the crisis, Alan Greenspan, his sagging, impish face supporting oversized spectacles, emerged to announce remedial interest rate cuts.

The markets loved him for it. The phrase 'Greenspan put' was coined to describe traders' confidence that Greenspan, who became known as 'The Maestro',[3] would always boost liquidity to prevent falls in asset prices following a shock. Over time, this lifted asset valuations, narrowed interest rate premiums on riskier loans, and led to lower pricing of risk generally. If a multitude of forces worked together to subdue economic volatility in the early 1990s, the 'Greenspan put' continued the calm throughout the latter 1990s and into the new millennium as asset prices rose and rose.

John Taylor, a Stanford University economist, makes the point that by keeping their interest rates low, US authorities caused interest rates in other countries to be lower than they would have been. This played a role in the swelling of the technology stock market bubble, as well as in the expansion of the housing bubble that began at the same time and continued well after the former had ended.[4]

Good Times

It takes two to tango through a loan contract. Central banks can't force people to borrow. As the optimism of the boom and mania develop, and asset prices rise above levels justified by expected returns, there needs to be some reason (or preferably more than one) that both the investor and the lender can grasp to explain why, this time, the laws of financial gravity are suspended.

The first great financial mania and crash of the modern global economy—the South Sea Bubble—was driven by the partial truth of the profits that could be generated from the enslavement of African people. The transportation of slaves to the Americas, the production there of commodities for export to Europe, and the supply of manufactured goods to Africa and the Americas was a new source of great wealth. The South Sea Company was formed in Britain to profit from this unscrupulous innovation and the bubble emerged from the exaggerated expectations that grew around the real prospects.[5]

Likewise, the productivity gains and high investment in the mass production of new consumer goods in the United States provided a kernel of truth to support the speculative boom of the roaring 1920s. The 'tech boom' in American financial markets in the 1990s similarly relied on a kernel of truth. Here it was the application of new information technologies and the brilliant success of some companies established to make and sell consumer products using them.

There was also a real basis for an Anglosphere assets boom in the economic growth that preceded the Great Crash of 2008. There was moderate prosperity in the developed world outside Japan. The high growth rate of China and of other developing countries that defined the Platinum Age filtered into Anglosphere economies through globalisation: the integration of global markets for goods, services, capital and professional labour.

The strong growth in economies that tended to save extra income turned out to have a bigger influence on global savings than the tendency of the Anglosphere to spend more than it earned. Even when the Federal Reserve and other Western central banks recognised that the boom was getting out of hand and raised short-term interest rates from 2004, long-term interest rates remained low in real terms. This underpinned investment everywhere and provided an especially powerful boost to housing in the United States, where most mortgage lending is based on long-term loans with fixed interest rates. The stream of money pouring into US bond markets from surplus countries prevented the long-term interest rates from rising. Greenspan called this the 'bond market conundrum'. Conundrum or not, it kept borrowers buoyant and asset prices booming.

A second rationalisation for rising prices was the high rate of immigration for all Anglosphere states. On average, 1.5 million people per annum poured into the United States through the 1990s. This number fell significantly following visa restrictions resulting from the September 11 terrorist attacks. However, the fall was limited by the strength in illegal immigrants at around 500 000 per year.[6] The total population has been growing by an average of around 3 million per year, or 1 per cent, since 1990.[7]

Population growth has also increased in the United Kingdom over recent decades. An average annual growth of 0.5 per cent since 2001 compares with 0.3 per cent between 1991 and 2001, and 0.2 per cent between 1981 and 1991.[8] The entrance of seven new states into the European Union in 2004 boosted the net UK immigration rates above 200 000 per annum.

In Australia, population growth averaged 1.2 per cent or 210 000 persons per annum between 1991 and 2000, then jumped to an average of 1.4 per cent or 272 500 persons per annum between 2001 and 2007. Net immigration accounted for a high proportion of the increase.[9]

High immigration levels and population growth helped to explain rising housing prices to market participants in the United States, the United Kingdom and Australia. But as economist Robert Shiller of Yale University explains, in reality this did not account for much at all of the historic revaluation of housing assets in the three countries.[10] There is no fundamental scarcity of land for housing, and the special value of urban land in choice locations has only a modest effect on the averages.

In the short term, the value of housing might be pushed up if construction lags behind demand. But there is no strong evidence of this being important during the boom. In the United States, dwelling construction actually outpaced demographic trends.[11]

In Australia over the period 1985–2009, an average of one residential dwelling was built per 1.75 new Australians. This rate of building is well in excess of the current average of 2.55 persons per occupied dwelling.[12] Steve Keen, an economist at Western Sydney University, makes the point that 'only if 30 per cent of new dwellings involved the demolition of existing properties—an improbably high number—would the rate of supply of new dwellings be running behind the rate of growth of population'.[13]

Crazy Times

High economic growth and an increasing population were not the only reasons embraced by market participants to convince themselves that nothing strange was happening as the boom in asset prices entered the stratosphere. Four other factors helped the good times become crazy times: one demographic, one financial, one political and one psychological.

Australia, the United States and the United Kingdom shared a population bulge owing to the baby boom that followed World War II. The oldest of this baby boom generation turned forty-five in 1990, with the other members following suit over the next fifteen years. The 45–55 age bracket in the labour force has the highest earnings, with the most discretionary income and capacity for investment and speculation. According to social researcher Bernard Salt, the prospect of baby boomer retirement 'drove a frenzy of property and equity investment. And why not? They had watched property and shares rise non-stop from the seventies. It was fool-proof retirement investment'.

Stock market prices responded accordingly through the 1990s. They received extra impetus from internet stock trading, which enabled individuals to directly trade shares at the push of a button. Price-to-earnings ratios in major indexes stretched dramatically. The Standard & Poor's 500 in the United States rose from an average ratio of 15.5 in 1990 to 32.6 in 1998, the highest level in history. A similar phenomenon was apparent in the UK's FTSE and Australia's All Ordinaries Index.

The number of US households that owned equities in 1989 was 30 million—by 1999 that number had leapt to 50 million,[14] and in 2005 it reached 57 million, despite net purchases falling considerably after the 'tech wreck' over the millennium. Total direct equity holdings for UK individuals were valued at £90 billion in 1990, but by 2000 that figure had grown to £290 billion; as in the US, the millennium bear markets significantly reduced holdings.[15] Australian equity ownership also rose dramatically, from 34 per cent of adults in 1997 to 54 per cent in 1999. The 'tech wreck' bear market knocked holdings down to 50 per cent in 2002, but households returned to set a new high of 55 per cent in 2004.[16]

This shift into share trading was historic. Yet it was small by comparison with the speculative enthusiasm directed at Anglosphere consumers' primary asset: houses. From 1995 to the various peaks in 2006–07, median house prices grew by a total of 139 per cent in the United States,[17] 261 per cent in the United Kingdom[18] and 169 per cent in Australia.[19]

Baby boomers' social habits also contributed to a growth in housing demand. Rising divorce rates and older parenthood forced down the average number of people per household. The US average of 2.63 persons per household in 1990 fell to 2.57 in 2006.[20] In the United Kingdom, the average dropped slightly from 2.5 persons in 1991 to 2.4 in 2003.[21] In Australia the average dropped from three persons per household in 1980 to 2.55 in 2006.[22]

However, the housing market was supercharged by a swing in perception away from home ownership for a roof over one's head, and towards home ownership as investment.

In Australia, the shift is apparent in the aggregate number of properties that were bought and sold per annum. In 1995, 316 355 properties changed hands. By 2003, the figure was 574 201, up 81.5 per cent in eight years. Sales dipped for several years before rising above half a million again in 2007.[23]

The swing towards housing speculation and investment was given a political boost when the US, UK and Australian governments altered capital gains tax laws within two years of one another. The changes made it much more advantageous to receive income from capital gains than from the sale of the services of one's brain or hands. The first changes were in the United States in 1997, when the Clinton administration cut the capital gains tax from 28 per cent to 20 per cent for high-income earners. The same package of reforms exempted houses from capital gains tax if the sale price was under $500 000. The United Kingdom followed in 1998, when Chancellor of the Exchequer Gordon Brown introduced his new 'Taper Relief' scheme, which cut capital gains tax more the longer a property was held. The total relief available cut the 40 per cent rate to 26 per cent. By 2006 investment loans accounted for 9 per cent of new mortgages.[24]

In 1999, the then conservative Australian Government reduced the capital gains tax by half—in the highest tax bracket, to 25 per cent. Investors voted with their wallets. In 1990 investment loans represented 16 per cent of Australian mortgages at $13 billion. By 1999, such loans had grown from a low base to $82 billion, or 29 per cent of total mortgage debt. Over the next nine years, investment property loans grew 378 per cent to $310 billion, or 31 per cent of total mortgage debt.[25]

As the housing bubbles emerged, credit was made available to a new class of borrower. In 1999 the Clinton administration sought to promote house ownership in lower income groups by loosening credit standard rules for the mortgage providers Fannie Mae and Freddie Mac.[26] By 2000, myriad new mortgages made it much easier for people on low incomes and with poor credit histories to borrow for housing. These included dedicated subprime loans with interest rates that were higher than regular loans but offered honeymoon periods, negative amortisation and interest rate resets; all shared the characteristic of a minimum or no deposit.

Through the 1990s, subprime constituted 9 per cent of total mortgage lending. By 2004, the ratio of subprime to new loans was 21 per cent. As the mania hit its peak, $600 billion of subprime loans were written in 2006 alone.[27] The bubble developed particularly in the coastal states of the south-western, south-eastern and north-western United States, where speculators (called flippers) took advantage of the zero-deposit loans to buy and sell properties with abandon.[28]

The United Kingdom also enjoyed a golden age of mortgage innovation. Credit standards declined there too but not as deeply as in the United States, where the sheer size of the market made it possible for specialist subprime lenders to flourish. Nonetheless, after the turn of the millennium, loans above 100 per cent of collateral value became available—by 2005, the ratio was extended to 125 per cent.[29]

Australian versions of 'non-conforming loans' finally arrived before the turn of the millennium and were soon in widespread use across the most conservative banks.

By the middle of the first decade of the twenty-first century, the psychology of the boom was well established. After multiple years of strong growth and rising asset values, risks seem to diminish in financial markets. The gambler has thrown the dice a number of times, and each time has won, while the investors who have remained cautious are less successful and fall from favour. Those

with money to lend or invest as equity in speculative
ventures watch the gambler throw and win, and begin to
think that he has skills beyond the ordinary human. The
gambler who borrows heavily for speculative investment,
the lender who accepts high margins for disproportionate
risk, and others who suspend the normal judgements of
prudence appear on the rich lists. They become responsible
for investing higher proportions of the world's capital.

The speculators become popular heroes and more
influential in political systems. Those in leadership positions who take seriously their responsibilities for impos-
ing constraints on the use by investors of other people's
money are pushed to the margins of public life. Some of
the prudent, including regulators, also come to believe
that risk is not what it used to be, and are less confident
of their old positions. If they make this transformation in
perception early enough, they retain their influence and
may even become maestros of a new financial order.

This is the eternal story of the bubble in capitalist
economies. Yale behavioural economist Robert Shiller
tells us that this process is a reflection of human
nature; it's a reflexive response, hard-wired into human
beings, part of their social make-up. To this we can
add the observations of economist Robert Aliber of the
University of Chicago, and Massachusetts Institute of
Technology economic historian Charles Kindleberger
in the updated fifth edition of the latter's classic history
Manias, Panics, and Crashes.[30] They observe that since
the 1970s, the world has seen a greater frequency and
amplitude of financial manias, and they attribute the

increasing instability to greater linkages of trade, finance and investment.

When more and more of the world is linked, the variations across countries develop closer connections and come to reinforce each other. The liberalisation of financial transactions seems to have left more scope for the herd to gain momentum in a boom, as well as in a panic, when the herd changes its course. Aliber and Kindleberger call this the dark side of globalisation.

3

Global Imbalances

ON 1 JUNE 2009, the US Secretary of the Treasury, Tim Geithner, returned to Peking University, where he had spent some time in his younger years. Geithner gave a speech on United States–China economic relations in a large auditorium before a crowd of students and teachers. Behind his lectern was a backdrop of Chinese and US flags that each stood some four metres high and were arranged side by side along a navy blue wall. Geithner cut a small figure on the stage, his red tie and thin features lost amidst the colourful drapery.

His speech was upbeat on the effect of policy responses to the Great Crash. But following his address, a single question from the audience made Geithner's diminutive presence the message of the day. A student inquired about the safety of China's holdings of US Treasury bonds. Geithner answered that 'Chinese assets are very safe', and was greeted with uproarious laughter from the crowd.

Two young Peking University staff members later explained that their laughter had been prompted by embarrassment over the question, and relief at Geithner's response. Others in the audience were displaying an old irreverence, a delight in the discomfort of the powerful. Chinese officials were familiar with this trait and had long been wary of the students at the country's most famous university.

So what had happened to reduce the holder of one of the world's most powerful economic policy offices to a bond salesman?

In the first few years of the twenty-first century, a great flood of surplus savings found its way from East Asia and resource exporting countries to the United States and the rest of the Anglosphere. As a proportion of these economies, the surpluses and deficits were the largest in modern history. The lending that flooded into the deficit countries allowed them to increase expenditure on housing, consumption and government, as well as to reduce taxation, beyond what would once have been regarded as prudent limits. The legacy of this debt was being visited upon Timothy Geithner in Beijing 2009.

For a number of years Australia had been the champion of the Anglosphere in high current account deficits and foreign debt as a proportion of GDP, with officials and many private economists maintaining that these did not matter in an economy with a floating currency so long as the deficits were generated in the private sector. There was no apparent problem with this growing indebtedness while the nation's banks had ready access to international credit on historically favourable terms. The old wariness of heavy foreign borrowing had been turned into a virtue: it was now said to show that international capital had confidence in investing in the country. There was a similarly dominant view in other deficit countries such as the United States and the United Kingdom, though it was usually qualified and challenged more than in Australia.

This was the flip-side of the rapidly growing surpluses of China and East Asia, and from the mid 2000s, the resource exporting countries.

For a time, both sides of the exchange seemed to receive great benefits from these global imbalances. But did these ultimately cause the Great Crash of 2008?

China's Way

What was behind the exceptionally large payments surpluses in East Asia and the resource exporting countries, all of which funded large deficits in the Anglosphere?

Financial Times economist Martin Wolf points to the lessons learned from the Asian Financial Crisis.[1] When the deficit countries required support from the International Monetary Fund (IMF), they were forced to accept humiliating conditions and counterproductive economic policies. That experience made countries across South-East Asia, as well as South Korea and China, determined never again to find themselves similarly exposed. They therefore ran cautious monetary and fiscal policies, holding domestic expenditure growth well below the rapidly increasing productive capacities of their economies.

Australian economist Max Corden adds that China's capacity to spend resources domestically is currently much lower than the resources available. It makes sense for the authorities to park money offshore, for use at a later time.[2]

Corden and Wolf both note that the Chinese tendency to hold real domestic expenditure below current incomes and output has involved elements of 'exchange rate protection'. Removing or reducing the surplus by expanding domestic expenditure or raising the yuan exchange rate against other currencies would have reduced the competitiveness of established export and import-competing industries. This would have been resisted politically by vested interests.

This is related to the popular foreign allegation that Chinese surpluses are the result of Chinese 'mercantilism'—a long-term tendency to artificially promote exports, resist imports and accumulate foreign reserves. This argument has it that the large surpluses of East Asia and some other economies cause global financial instability. The economically sophisticated version of the allegation says that increases in savings relative to investment in East Asia, and particularly China, meant that other countries, such as those in the Anglosphere, had to increase their expenditure to avoid an excess of capacity globally, and a downturn in global incomes and employment.

But there is a different, bigger story about the extraordinary growth of savings in China, and the excess of savings over investment that was reflected in the current account surplus.

We need to recognise that these large surpluses are recent phenomena. The Chinese external accounts fluctuated widely over the first one and a half decades of reform to the mid 1990s. Periods of surplus were interrupted by periods of deficit. Then, during the Asian Financial Crisis at the end of the decade, the growth of exports slowed much more than imports. Speculators found ways of moving capital out of China. Chinese officials and external commentators alike wondered whether it would be possible to hold the fixed exchange rate of the yuan against the dollar, or whether the growing payments deficit and loss of reserves would force the currency to fall in value. After the financial crisis, in 2001, the surplus was still only 1.3 per cent of GDP; by 2007, it had grown to 11 per cent.[3]

So if there is a Chinese mercantilism, it is recent in origin.

The Asian Financial Crisis did induce caution in East Asian developing countries about exposure to the whims of the global financial markets. But for China, the story of external pressures and policy responses from 1997 to 2000 was largely reassuring. Chinese authorities were under great pressure from financial markets to lower the value of the yuan against the dollar, but they decided to hold the exchange rate constant. This meant that it increased in value by a large amount against the currencies of most other countries, including Japan and other East Asian economies, and Australia and other commodity exporting countries. At the same time, China implemented large-scale Keynesian fiscal expansion to offset the contractionary effects of falling exports.

The rationale for the approach had both domestic and international elements. At home, and most importantly, it maintained employment and incomes while avoiding greater risks of financial instability. Abroad, it helped to break the downward cycle of contraction of economic output, falling currency and shrinking imports into which the East Asian region had descended.

The Chinese economic strategy throughout the financial crisis included acceptance of a payments deficit. It was risky, but successful. The episode increased Chinese confidence in managing large external shocks, and in particular shocks from reduced exports in the context of international financial crises.

Growth of Chinese exports and output surged through the post-millennium boom, taking Chinese officials and foreign analysts by surprise. The numbers exceeded official budgets and forecasts in every year from 2001 to 2008. Imports also grew more strongly than anticipated, but not to the same extent. As a result, the current account surplus increased explosively and unexpectedly.

Since the early 1990s, export growth has been spurred by three factors: increases in productivity associated with reform, and high levels of domestic and especially direct foreign investment; deeper integration into global goods and services markets after Chinese entry into the World Trade Organization in 2001; and a steady exchange rate against the US dollar from 1994 until July 2005.

The foreign exchange inflow was augmented beyond the large current account surpluses by high levels of direct foreign investment. From about 2005, speculative capital inflows also became important. Characteristically, these inflows accelerated from July in that year after China began to appreciate its currency because it created what speculators saw as a one-way bet.

Foreign exchange reserves rose to higher levels than had ever been known for a single country: from $166 billion in 2000 to $1946 billion in December 2008.[4]

We can present this same information differently by focusing on the gap between savings and investment rather than on the one between exports and imports. The surplus of savings over investment has to equal the surplus of exports over imports. Chinese savings and investment rates had both been exceptionally high and rising through the reform period. Both grew substantially more strongly than GDP in the early twenty-first century, but savings grew even more rapidly than investment. The savings, therefore, need more explanation than the investment rates. The question of why investment was 'so low' is not in such urgent need of an answer since the investment shares of output and expenditure are higher than they have ever been on a sustained basis in any country bigger than Singapore.

There were contributions to higher savings from the government, business and household sectors. In government, there was substantial fiscal consolidation after the Keynesian expansion in 1998–2000 raised budget deficits to high levels. In the business sector, there was a strong focus on raising the commercial performance of state-owned enterprises. This was generally successful. Profitability of enterprises was raised by full or partial privatisation, with full privatisation being more common in the years following the Asian Financial Crisis.[5] For firms that continued to be owned by the state, a range of measures was directed at improving commercial performance. Much of the increase in earnings was retained within the enterprises, contributing to both high national savings and investment.

The weakness in general social security arrangements is often cited as one reason for household savings being high. The lack of a social 'safety net' encouraged citizens to make private provision for sickness, unemployment and old age. This is especially significant in a labour force that is ageing rapidly. The limited availability of financial services to support consumption, especially in comparison with the Anglosphere, is also important.

Incomes grew so fast in China that patterns of consumer behaviour did not keep pace. A variation on this idea is familiar from Keynesian macro-economics in the West, where it was known as the Duesenberry hypothesis. Consumption adjusts to consumers' expectations of sustainable incomes. Recent increases in incomes were not thought to be sustainable with certainty. But even to the extent that they were, consumers took time to learn and accept radically new patterns of consumption. This consideration was important in Japan and other East Asian economies during rapid growth. It has been important in India, where savings rates have risen rapidly in the reform era, despite income growing significantly more slowly than in China.

In contemporary China, many people see advantages in being self-employed—in owning a small business that hopefully becomes a large business. This carries prestige and the possibility of some negotiated independence from the state. Many Chinese are prepared to forego consumption to secure and enhance this status. Business investment to some extent competes with consumption in the household budget.

Of the various contributions to savings, the retained earnings of business investment was the largest.

All of these factors help to explain exceptionally high savings rates without giving weight to the authorities' desire to remain beyond the reach of the IMF.

Savings Glut

China contributed more than all other surplus countries combined to the increased surplus savings of the first decade of the twenty-first century. Japan and Germany continued to contribute surplus savings for international investment. But these were constants within global payments imbalances over this period. Other Asian developing countries made more substantial contributions to the changes. India had much in common with China but on a smaller scale.

Once the post-millennium boom took hold, the other large shift that contributed to global imbalances was the much higher savings and current account surpluses of the commodity exporting countries. The Organisation of the Petroleum Exporting Countries (OPEC) and Russia in particular experienced terms-of-trade booms after commodity prices began to rise strongly from 2003. Much of the increase was temporary. The exceptionally high commodity prices lasted until the second half of 2008.

The fiscal policies of many resource exporting countries were designed to hold back some of the revenue from higher export prices, to avoid a domestic expansion that would be so large that it would require retrenchment when prices returned to more normal levels. They were applying a lesson learnt from earlier episodes of high commodity prices. In addition, some governments accumulated reserves because they needed time to plan and implement effective expenditure programs.

These factors collectively meant that a rising tide of surplus savings was available for international investment over the years from the turn of the century to the onset of the Great Crash. This was the mirror image of the rapidly rising deficits in the Anglosphere.

In the United States, the government surpluses of the late 1990s were replaced after 2000 by budget deficits that commenced in the shallow recession of the 'tech wreck' but extended through the period of moderate growth that followed. Increased government expenditure on defence and cuts in taxation rates were major contributors. Household savings fell to around zero at the same time as housing investment reached unusually high levels.

In the United Kingdom and Australia, lower household savings interacted with a boom in housing investment to produce a large deficit. Australia's case was particularly interesting. It enjoyed a large increase in incomes as a resource exporting country from about 2004. Household savings were negative from 2002 into 2006, at times to more than 3 per cent of income.[6] Business investment rose more than business savings, adding to the large borrowing requirements in the household sector. Australian governments increased expenditure at historically high rates and reduced taxation, yet the revenue increases were so large that they also ran Budget surpluses. But these were overwhelmed by much larger private sector deficits.

The surpluses in some countries must equal the deficits in others. How did the economic conditions in

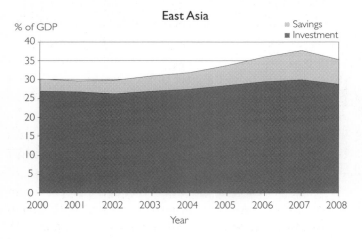

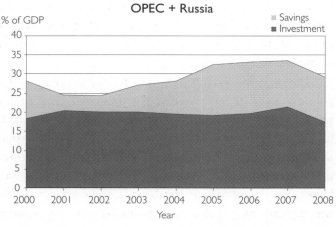

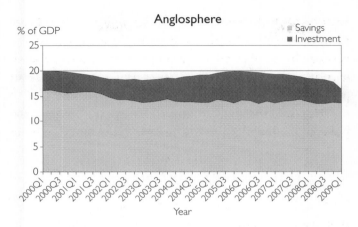

Source: Euromonitor International from International Monetary Fund (IMF),
International Financial Statistics (annual data)

the surplus countries interact with those in the deficit
countries to produce the outcomes described above?

The policies and behaviours in the Anglosphere supported strong growth in incomes, exports and savings in
the surplus countries. They also supported strong growth
in exports of consumer goods of increasing variety and
sophistication. They underwrote an easy option for continued strong economic growth, without any change in
economic strategy or structure.

The surplus savings of East Asia and later of the
resource exporters supported the preferred policies and
patterns of growth of the Anglosphere. Tax cuts and
higher public expenditure on the scale of the Anglosphere
in the early twenty-first century might have been expected
to raise interest rates considerably. This, in turn, would
have been expected to inhibit the implementation of
the expansionary policies. The availability of abundant

funding from abroad allowed high expenditures to be pursued without constraint or inhibition.

Surplus and deficit nations independently chose policies that increased global imbalances. Each benefited for a while from the policies of the other. Each was able to avoid rethinking policies and strategies that introduced risks and vulnerabilities for people everywhere.

Why Imbalances Matter

For the world as a whole, savings must equal investment. If there is a tendency for the sum of the surpluses to exceed the sum of the deficits, global long-term interest rates fall. This encourages expenditure, consumption and investment in all countries. The reduction in savings and the increase in investment induced by the fall in interest rates brings realised global savings into line with realised investments.

The rapid growth of countries with tendencies towards surplus, such as China in the post-millennium boom, tends to reduce global interest rates and to increase global investment. The increased investment is in itself favourable to global economic growth, especially in capital-scarce developing countries.

If we had a single world governed as one entity in which total savings were in balance with total investment at full employment, and drew lines on a map to define countries, some would have payments surpluses, and some deficits. All would have levels of surpluses and deficits that raised their people's welfare to the maximum possible level. No-one would think the imbalances important.

But these imbalances are significant. First, there is a tendency for investors to segment the world into countries in their assessment of opportunities and risk. When things go wrong and suppliers are more cautious, they tend to pull back first and most strongly from foreign countries. Second, countries have independent mechanisms for setting monetary, fiscal and trade policies that can affect the way in which imbalances interact with the real economy. These mechanisms tend to favour national over foreign businesses, especially in times of economic instability.

Third, and perhaps most importantly for an understanding of the Great Crash, international imbalances are only sustainable so long as there are institutions that can provide easy, cost-effective movement of capital. Only trustworthy banks and financial institutions can transfer funds from the surplus savers to the deficit borrowers. These are less likely to be available for movement of capital between countries than within them. Once the established global banks ran into trouble, both halves of the global imbalances were exposed to drastic economic corrections.

The imbalances helped to set the scene for the Great Crash of 2008 by facilitating the assets boom beyond the point where constraints were otherwise likely to have been imposed. Then, as the shifting of savings from surplus to deficit countries suddenly collapsed, they ensured that the Great Crash became the Great Recession.

4

Clever Money

IN 2006, JOHN KENNETH Galbraith, the grand witness to the Great Crash of 1929, departed this earth for that place in heaven that is reserved for readable economists. One can imagine him looking down and rolling his eyes at the vast and fantastic array of new financial instruments known as derivatives created over the decade before the Great Crash of 2008.

In his 1990 book *A Short History of Financial Euphoria*, Galbraith summed up financial innovation through the ages:

> Financial operations do not lend themselves to innovation. What is recurrently so described and celebrated is, without exception, a small variation on an established design ... The world of finance hails the invention of the wheel over and over again, often in a slightly more unstable version.[1]

The so-called innovations known as derivatives allowed imbalances in the global economy to be much greater than would have been the case under the old rules. They enabled banks to dramatically increase their leverage and gave individuals and businesses access to credit they could never repay. Entire nations were freed to live beyond their means. When the breaking of the old rules reached its inevitable conclusion, the world was left with shattered trust in its financial system.

Since the mid 1980s, credit creation in much of the world has been transformed by a complex of hedge funds, money-market funds and investment banks dubbed the 'shadow banking' system.[2] Like traditional banks, the shadow banking system shifts capital from those with savings to those who want to borrow. It does so using a range of market-based derivative products that help to manage credit and interest rate risk, and which have been celebrated by many as a productive revolution in banking.

Traditional banks borrow short-term funds in the form of customer deposits in return for interest and the return of principal. They then use the money to make loans of longer duration, such as mortgages and personal or business loans. They take clearly identified assets as security in case of default. To guard against insolvency, the banks are required by law to hold enough capital in reserve in the event of loss. The ratio of loans a bank makes against this capital is called its leverage and is controlled by regulators.

Also supporting the system is a central bank that supplies money in the event that depositors want their money back more quickly than the banks can supply it.

This might be necessary in the event of a run by depositors, or in a 'panic'. The US Government offers further support by guaranteeing the return of deposits through the Federal Deposit Insurance Corporation.

The shadow banking system raises money directly from investors, traditional banks or other shadow banks rather than taking deposits. Because there are no deposits in the forms subject to traditional regulation, operations are hidden from regulators. Shadow banks are not required to hold capital reserves and therefore can use higher levels of leverage. The system has no support from a central bank. In other words, shadow banks often take greater risks than traditional banks, but without the regulatory requirements and prudential supervision.

Heading up to the Great Crash, there was no clear separation between shadow banks and traditional banks. Shadow banking was as much a method of creating credit as it was a discrete system. As early as the mid 1990s, more than 80 per cent of US lending was conducted by or channelled through the shadow banking system.[3]

Deposit-taking banks became responsible for the creation of some of shadow banking's most problematic methods and products. It was a team of credit analysts at JPMorgan who invented the credit default swap (CDS). And it was Citigroup that was the most aggressive pioneer of the use of short-term forms of debt to fund what were thought to be safe long-term securities such as collateralised debt obligations (CDOs).[4]

Shadow Banking and Securitisation

So what exactly is shadow banking and how did it come about?

Shadow banking can be categorised in three ways. The first is the shadow banking system itself: the many different financial firms that conduct the business. These include investment banks, hedge funds, money-market funds, monoline insurers, mortgage originators (called non-bank lenders in Australia) and rating agencies. They are invisible to regulators and use, or enable others to use, risk-shifting derivatives instead of using capital reserves to manage possible losses.

The second category is the use of shadow banking methods by traditional deposit-taking banks. These continue to operate under regulatory scrutiny and have the central bank support that comes with that, but they also participate in shadow banking methods in parts of their business.

The third category covers the instruments of shadow banking. These are the derivative products that enable institutions to shift risk, increase leverage and operate beyond regulatory scrutiny.

Securitisation, the most important banking process of the past fifteen years, crosses over these three categories. Securitisation is a practice through which an illiquid but income-producing asset, such as a mortgage, is converted into a security that is more easily traded by investors. Our story of how shadow banking evolved starts here.

The seeds of securitisation were sown during the Great Depression when, as part of the New Deal,

Franklin Delano Roosevelt created the Federal National Mortgage Association, or Fannie Mae. Fannie Mae was a government business that carried the AAA government credit rating and could raise money cheaply by borrowing cash from investors in the form of bonds. It used the proceeds from the bonds to buy mortgages from banks. The difference between the interest rate that Fannie Mae paid on its bonds and the interest rate it received on its mortgages, known as the spread, covered Fannie Mae's costs and generated its profit. Through this set of transactions, Fannie Mae effectively converted mortgages—which are not readily tradable—into liquid bonds, or securities, that investors would trade.

The buying of mortgages from banks created what was known as the secondary mortgage market. For fifty years, Fannie Mae successfully increased the funds available to US borrowers for housing through this market. Fannie Mae was privatised in 1968, and in 1970 it was joined by a similar firm: the Federal Home Loan Mortgage Corporation, or Freddie Mac. Even after privatisation, their bonds were perceived to retain the government guarantee. They both became known as government-sponsored enterprises (GSEs).

In the early 1970s, the GSEs invented a more complex method for securitising the mortgages they had purchased from banks. Rather than hold the mortgages until maturity themselves, they pooled them, then split the pool into shares called mortgage-backed securities (MBS). These securities were effectively bonds that directly funded the mortgages in the pools, but they did so at arms-length from Fannie Mae and Freddie Mac. The MBS retained the perception of a government AAA rating, and conservative investors were comfortable buying them. By doing this, both associations still channelled investor funds into the mortgages, but shifted the risk off their books and onto the investment entity that managed the pool. This meant they no longer needed to hold capital in reserve against the mortgages. They could use it instead to buy more mortgages. From 1985 to 2007, the GSE MBS market grew from $367.9 billion to $4.46 trillion.[5]

Wall Street investment banks began to tap into the booming secondary mortgage market in the early 1980s, but the traders faced a problem. They could not replicate the Fannie Mae and Freddie Mac business model because conservative investors demanded securities with AAA ratings, like those provided by the GSEs. To get around this, traders devised ingenious new methods to enhance the credit ratings of their mortgage bonds.

The investment banks formed structured investment vehicles (SIVs). These were subsidiaries that had no claim on the parent balance sheet and existed beyond regulatory restrictions on leverage. The SIV borrowed to buy mortgages in the secondary market and pool them. The combined cash flows were then separated into segments or 'tranches'. Each tranche sliced a variety of different mortgages to create different levels of risk. The lowest-risk tranches were given AAA ratings and the investment banks offered to sell these to the same set of conservative investors that liked Fannie Mae and Freddie Mac bonds: superannuation funds, governments and foreign government entities. And sell they did. From 1985 to 2007, the private MBS market run by the banks grew from $24.7 billion to $2.96 trillion.[6]

Before long, investment banks realised that the same process could just as easily apply to any set of fixed-income assets. In 1985, the first securitisation of car loans took place. The following year it was credit card loans. The process of creating and selling these rapidly expanding forms of securitisation became known as 'asset-backed finance'.[7]

In 1988, several regulatory shifts strapped securitisation and the asset-backed securities (ABS) market to a rocket. The first occurred when the Group of 10 nations, comprising Belgium, Canada, France, Germany, Italy, Japan, the Netherlands, Sweden, Switzerland, the United Kingdom and the United States, met in Basel, Switzerland, to draft a set of rules to govern capital reserve requirements for global banking. The meeting was known as the Basel Committee and the Accord that resulted was called Basel I.

Basel I was meant to strengthen prudential arrangements for an increasingly global financial system. Basel I strictly defined the risk associated with various types of loans. It also provided rules that directed banks to hold certain levels of capital in reserve against the different loan types. For instance, lending to corporations demanded an 8 per cent capital reserve, while lending for mortgages required half that because the risk of default was considered to be lower.

Some banks criticised the Basel I rules for being excessively restrictive because risk was based only on the category of borrowing. The bank therefore had to hold the same amount of capital in reserve regardless of the credit-worthiness of the borrower.[8] Investment banks turned to securitisation to get around these limits. Because securiti-sation meant that the loans were removed from the bal-ance sheet, no capital was required to be held in reserve.

The second regulatory shift occurred within the United States. It enabled traditional banks to enter the securiti-sation market and compete with the investment banks. Under pressure from Chase Manhattan Bank, the Federal Reserve allowed deposit-taking banks to underwrite cer-tain securities for the first time since Congress had passed the Glass-Steagall Act. This was Great Depression–era legislation that prevented deposit-taking banks from conducting securities business. Glass-Steagall had been enacted to preclude various practices that were thought to have contributed to the crisis of the 1930s.

Initially, traditional banks were only allowed to draw up to 5 per cent of their total revenues from these sources. But after lobbying by JPMorgan, Chase Manhattan, Bankers Trust and Citicorp, the range of securities that could be underwritten was expanded in 1989 and 1990, and the limit raised to 10 per cent of revenues. This was when traditional banks began using shadow banking methods.[9]

As the players expanded, so did the market. In the 1990s, asset-backed finance broadened to include securities backed by corporate bonds, life insurance premiums, catastrophe insurance premiums, toll roads revenues, even David Bowie's record royalties—any asset with an apparently steady cash flow was fair game.[10] In

1996 the US Federal Reserve raised its limit on the revenues
of traditional banks to 25 per cent. In the subsequent
decade the stunning growth of ABS continued.

 According to the New York Federal Reserve, by 2007

> Asset-backed commercial paper conduits, in struc-
> tured investment vehicles, in auction-rate preferred
> securities, tender option bonds and variable rate
> demand notes, had a combined asset size of roughly
> $2.2 trillion. Assets financed overnight in triparty
> repo grew to $2.5 trillion. Assets held in hedge
> funds grew to roughly $1.8 trillion. The combined
> balance sheets of the then five major investment
> banks totaled $4 trillion.[11]

The investment banks that defined shadow banking
and the traditional banks that used the system's methods
had all successfully intensified the use of their capital
and avoided Basel I. But eventually, all of the banks
involved in ABS faced a new problem. The securitisation
process shifts and repackages risk. It does not eliminate
it. Therefore, when risk was shifted to create a low-risk
tranche, it always left behind the securities of the residual
tranche with commensurately higher risk. Because the
banks were unable to sell all of these low-rated, high-
risk securities to investors, they wallowed on the balance
sheets of the SIVs, or on their own balance sheets.

 The rise of securitisation and its problems were
part of the reason that the Basel Committee met again
in 1999. The new Accord that resulted, known as Basel
II, gave banks greater discretion in weighing the risk for
any individual loan. The allocation of capital against the

risk-weighted value of assets became a process of internal risk assessment. Investors were therefore more reliant on private rating agencies for assurance that the banks had weighed the credit risk of their securities correctly. The Accord was not scheduled for full implementation until 2008, but regulators began preparing and implementing parts of it much earlier.

With the early twenty-first century boom underway, interest rates at historic lows, and the rating agencies enjoying bigger roles, investment and traditional banks involved in ABS realised that they could also now use securitisation to make money from the residual high-risk tranches. These were bundled into new pools, sometimes with other securities, and then chopped up into new tranches. The top level of these new tranches had the first right to cash flows from the underlying securities, so it was assumed that unless all of the underlying mortgage-backed securities went bust at once, the investment was still very safe. Known as collateralised debt obligations (CDOs), these new securities were again granted AAA investment ratings and were sold around the world to conservative investors.

Of course, this process also left Wall Street banks holding the commensurately higher-risk tranches that they were unable to sell. 'No problem', they said. 'We'll securitise those too.' And so they did, pooling the low-rated, high-risk, residual CDOs and again obtaining AAA ratings for the top tranche cut from the pools, which they then sold. These became known as CDO^2.

Extraordinarily, another round of securitisation was worked upon the residual high-risk tranches of CDO^2

and produced CDO^3. In the end, during the subprime mortgage boom, investors were being offered AAA-rated shares in the top tranche of a pool of residual high-risk CDO^2 tranches that had been cut from a pool of residual high-risk CDO tranches that had been cut from a pool of residual high-risk MBS tranches that were themselves underpinned by America's highest-risk mortgages and other loans!

Many of those who bought the various forms of CDO say that they had no idea what it was that they were actually funding. This applies to the A\$625.6 million invested by Australian councils and community groups in Lehman Brothers securities, one of the investment banks heavily engaged in ABS.[12]

Nonetheless, the high yields and hidden risks of residual tranches based on subprime loans made CDOs very attractive in a period of low interest rates. Demand tended to outstrip supply. In response, by 2005 traders were using derivatives that bet on the credit performance of CDOs, which were then bundled into new products. This new peak in baroque finance was called a synthetic CDO. Because it didn't actually define ownership of anything, the synthetic CDOs could be re-created ad infinitum. 'That's how you took a small portion of the residential mortgage market and went around the world to lose 15 times as much', said Phoebe Moreo, a partner in the US office of Deloitte & Touche's securitisation transactions team.[13]

Despite the efforts made to repackage and shift risk, there was always an increasingly toxic residual tranche and its associated securities. For years, the investment and traditional banks using securitisation hid these concentrated slices of financial dark matter. According to journalist Corine Hegland of the *National Journal*, they did so by 'either pretending they had voluntarily purchased the leftovers to resell later, or by thrusting them into the short-term debt [money] markets in the guise of top-grade, AAA-rated, asset-backed commercial paper'.[14]

When the money markets that were supplying the debt began waking up to reality in September 2007, they refused to roll over the loans underpinning the SIVs. This was the moment of crisis. The many high-risk residual securities that the banks had juggled between the SIVs and money-market funds were suddenly forced back onto parent bank balance sheets. The banks' capital ratios were now too low. These are the famous toxic assets that paralysed US banking—$1 trillion of them.

Other Shadows

As the story of the shadow banking system and its methods suggests, the investment banks and their traditional bank rivals did not pull securitisation together all by themselves. Other players were needed to make it work. First of all, the investment banks either purchased mortgages from non-bank mortgage originators (non-bank lenders) or bought the originators outright. These were the retail outlets of shadow banking, lending money to consumers but holding no deposits. After the creation of the securitisation process in the United States in the early 1980s, mortgage originators grew at an astounding pace. The National Association of Mortgage Brokers estimated that in 2004 there were 53 000 mortgage brokers employing 418 700 people.[15]

Splitting the origination of loans from their financing introduced a new set of incentives at the retail end of the chain. Since the non-bank has no intention of retaining the mortgage on its balance sheet, it has far less motivation to consider the credit quality of the borrower for the future. Worse, since its revenue now derives from fees for originating the loan, rather than cash flows from the loan itself, it is motivated to produce as many loans as possible, no matter what the chance of the loan being repaid. This led to fraudulent appraisals, misstatements of income and generally lax underwriting.[16]

The relaxation of standards helped push US house ownership from 64 per cent in 1994 to a peak of 69 per cent in 2004. It was a principal cause of the subprime boom, the collapse of which would trigger the Great Crash.

Deteriorating loan quality was not a problem for the new shadow bank system. In one way, it made things even better. Since a low-quality borrower pays a higher interest rate, there was more spread for the securitisation chain to monetise. Besides, another shadow banking player would step in where necessary to boost credit quality. Enter the monoline insurance companies, firms that lend their own AAA rating to the bonds of another firm in return for a fee. This process is known as 'insurance wrapping'.

Several major monoline firms were heavily involved in insurance wrapping MBS and CDO products. The most famous of these was the financial products line of the world's biggest insurance company, American Insurance Group (AIG). These firms were all involved in insuring various stages of the securitisation process, sometimes selling a guarantee known as a credit default swap (CDS). A bank would pay a fee and in return the monoline guaranteed that, in the event of a part or full default on a given MBS or CDO, it would cover the losses. This lent critical AAA support to the securitisation process.

And there were other players too. According to the *Financial Times*:

> Hedge funds often provided the equity at the foundations of this system and illustrate why shadow banking had such an outsized impact on the supply of credit. Satyajit Das, an author and derivatives industry expert, cites an example where just $10m of real, unlevered hedge fund money supported an $850m mortgage-backed deal. This means $1 of real money was used to create $85 of mortgage lending. Credit creation far beyond the wildest dreams of high-street bankers.[17]

With such multiples of capital available, traditional banks increasingly used shadow banking methods through the creation of their own SIVs.

Two other players were crucial to the success of the system. Once established, an SIV borrowed heavily to purchase the mortgages to be securitised. This debt came from short-term lenders called money-market funds. Investors in money-market funds include schools, hospitals, pension funds and corporations that need to park cash in the short term. The funds are restricted to the most secure investments, those with less than 13-month maturities according to the US Securities and Exchange Commission's (SEC) Investment Company Act of 1940. To borrow from these funds, SIVs needed the AAA low-risk stamp of approval of the rating agencies: Moody's, Fitch and Standard & Poor's. This ensured that the high-ratings monoline insurers reappeared to credit-wrap the debt and guarantee the ratings.

The risk for the ratings was determined on the basis of historical analysis of the probabilities of defaults and losses across the shadow banking system. Given that the system had only a limited history of operation through business cycles, these assumptions were courageous to say the least. It was this fallacy of induction that Nassim Taleb attacked so compellingly before the crash in his best-selling book *The Black Swan*. The problems of inductive reasoning were compounded by a flaw in statistical analysis that was common in the financial theory of the times: a presumption that the possible outcomes from risky activities would follow a 'normal' distribution.

It seems that the operational methods of the rating agencies were also suspect. A 2008 SEC investigation of how the agencies went about assessing the risk in subprime MBS and CDOs concluded that the agencies never looked at a single loan file of the millions that underpinned the securities. When the investigation examined a random cross-section of the loan files, there was the appearance of fraud in almost every one.[18] The rating agency Fitch described the result as 'disconcerting'.[19]

The same SEC investigation reported an exchange between two analysts at a rating agency. The analysts were discussing whether they should be rating a particular deal. One expressed concern that her firm's model did not capture 'half' of the deal's risk, but that 'it could be structured by cows and we would rate it'.[20]

It is not difficult to find the motive behind the deteriorating standards. Agencies were locked in a growing conflict of interest. For instance, by 2006, 40 per cent of Moody's earnings were coming directly from fees related to rating ABS. The fees were paid by the banks that issued the securities, not the investors who bought them.[21] The rating agencies were the linchpin in a shadow banking scheme designed to generate AAA ratings without the responsibility of setting aside capital to back up the ratings.

Writing in the *Financial Times* in March 2009, US insurance regulator Eric Dinallo described the shadow banking system as a failed attempt to create a new asset class that guaranteed investor returns without the capital provisions that make such guarantees substantive.[22] Also in March 2009, William Black, Associate Professor of Economics and Law at the University of Michigan, and a regulator during the savings and loan crisis, stated in a Public Broadcasting Service interview that the peculiar self-reference that allowed the thin capital provisions was simply part of a gargantuan fraud by all concerned.[23]

Whether or not Black is right about malfeasance is not the most important thing. More salient is the truth that the US securitisation process and its accompanying derivatives stretched the rules governing transactions past breaking point. The borrower was separated from the lender, the lender from ownership, AAA guarantees from capital provisions, profit centres from balance sheets, risk from reward, and the process of credit creation from oversight. Into each of these fissures slipped a specialist provider who received fees for services dependent upon the next specialist in the chain, with no incentive to question the quality or sustainability of the pass-through product.

It was a system based on liquidity, the belief that risk-shifting could supplant real capital reserves, and the confidence that there was always another buyer. When the test came, it collapsed upon itself like a dying star.

Australian Shadow Banking

As in the United States, for much of the twentieth century Australian banking operated under a regulatory regime that separated traditional deposit-taking banks and investment banks. The deposit-taking banks had the support of the central bank as lender of last resort, and conservative capital reserve requirements. The separation of traditional banks from other financial institutions ended in 1983 as part of a wave of deregulation that also saw the issuing of many new banking licences to foreign-owned banks, as well as the liberalising of rules for other competitors such as building societies. However, unlike the United States, following deregulation the Australian authorities made efforts to extend the regulatory framework surrounding traditional banks to the new financial institutions.

An Australian shadow banking system did not emerge right away. It took government intervention to get the securitisation process going. In 1986, the New South Wales Government sponsored the formation of the First Australian National Mortgage Acceptance Corporation. At the same time, the Victorian Government established the National Mortgage Market Corporation. Both operations were subject to 26 per cent government ownership, with the remainder spread among a range of shadow bank players, including investment banks, building societies and unit trust managers. Not to be outdone, the Queensland Government legislated the *Secondary Mortgage Market Act* to support a program for 'originators' in that state. One private provider was also founded to compete with the new government lending shops: MGICA Securities, a subsidiary of AMP Ltd.

These early initiatives came to grief in the bond market meltdown in the lead-up to the recession of 1990–91. The government operations in particular were hit hard because they had exposed themselves to a huge refinancing risk. The NSW and Victorian operations were ultimately sold to the private sector; the Queensland market was stillborn. The shadow banking phoenix rose from these ashes in 1992 when John Symond founded Aussie Home Loans with the backing of Macquarie Bank, and John Kinghorn launched RAMS.

As with non-bank lenders in the United States, Aussie Home Loans and RAMS relied on investment banks to manage the securitisation process. From the mid 1990s they generated securities similar to the Wall Street MBS, called residential mortgage-backed securities (RMBS).

The securities were generally bought by a mix of local and foreign investors. They were extraordinarily successful, seizing 7 per cent of the outstanding mortgage market by 2006.

The non-bank lenders had no regulator and only light rules within fair trading and corporate law. And with investors globally becoming more accustomed to shadow banking, the standards that determined which Australians were creditworthy began to erode. The shadow bank lenders first introduced low-documentation or 'low-doc' loans in 1997, then 'no-doc' loans by 1999. Subprime or 'non-conforming' loans, given to people with bad or impaired credit histories, also proliferated in the late 1990s. Subprime specialist non-bank lenders such as Liberty Financial and Bluestone grew swiftly and issued subprime RMBS. These securities first appeared in 2000 and by the end of 2006 some A\$6.8 billion had been sold. The market was growing at 150 per cent per annum and looked set to burgeon.

A growing network of mortgage brokers held no deposits, had no reputational risk with investors and were paid in part by fees for mortgage volume. Amidst the rising arrears rates for Australian RMBS, the highest levels of default were apparent within broker-originated loans. Many of the industry participants interviewed for this book describe widespread fraud in underwriting standards managed by brokers. Endemic malpractices included getting clients to sign blank declarations of affordability (and income if relevant) and then working back to how much the client needed to earn to afford the loan.

When the market was in its mania, there was little subtlety in this practice. Audits of the files would readily demonstrate differences in handwriting. Some remarkable outcomes eventuated. Elderly applicants, either retired or in blue-collar occupations, were claiming to have extraordinarily high incomes. GE Money introduced what it called a 'sanity test' to forestall these types of occurrences in 2005. Another trick in the fraudster's handbook was to put up the application as an investment loan (therefore getting the benefit of the potential rental income to augment serviceability) when it was clear that the application was actually for owner occupation. This went hand in hand with the practice of 'necking kids'; that is, not declaring dependants to increase the applicants' available income.

In 2007, the Federal Court ordered one mortgage broker to pay a former client A$32 000 in compensation after the broker falsified documents to ensure a A$365 000 mortgage for the 20-year-old, unemployed, dyslexic and homeless man. The same broker was in court for similar abuses in 2009.[24]

According to Kym Dalton, former CEO of MGICA, Australia's first private mortgage originator, collapsing credit standards were also the result of another shadow bank player, the lenders mortgage insurance (LMI) provider:

> The 'dirty little secret' of the exponential growth of securitisation and RMBS in particular, is the role and complicity of the Lenders Mortgage Insurance providers. The banks historically only insured

loans that had less than a 20 per cent deposit and therefore there was an element of 'selecting against' the insurers in their use of the product. With the advent of the mortgage management sector and the likes of Aussie, RAMS and latterly, Wizard, the insurers had clients who insured every loan and therefore they got a 'spread of risk'. Combine this with the excessive exuberance of the most recent debt binge and one had the LMI providers often leading the way on a loosening of credit standards and an increase in risk. Brokers and mortgage managers being what they are, took the LMI's enthusiasm as licence to push the envelope and the 'feeling' ensued that the LMI policy was an 'indemnity' rather than a contract, as it is.

The business was dominated by the subsidiaries of two US companies: Genworth and PMI. The two firms split the various forms of mortgage insurance for Australian shadow banks almost down the middle. Typically, they insured the banks against default losses for individual high-risk borrowers or entire pools of mortgages set for securitisation.

To state the obvious, the concentration within the industry is not a diffusion of risk. Fortunately, LMIs are regulated. In 2005, the Australian Prudential Regulation Authority (APRA) conducted stress tests on the LMI sector, concluding: 'The result of applying the stress test on LMIs (monolines) revealed that LMIs would not fare as well as ADIs (Authorised Deposit taking Institutions) should the modeled stress event occur, and that APRA's minimum capital requirement for LMIs was inadequate'.

Capital reserve ratios were subsequently boosted. However, according to a March 2009 UBS report, the high concentration of the market and rising defaults still represent a risk of insolvency for Genworth and PMI.[25] If the worst happens, then the parent firms—Genworth US and QBE—may have to bail out their subsidiaries. Genworth's US parent has its own problems. The owner-ship compounds the systemic risk.

Australia's emerging shadow bank system was not as separate from traditional banks as appeared to be the case. Traditional banks supported the non-bank lenders by providing warehousing services for mortgages before they were securitised. For a fee, the banks held the mortgages on their balance sheets until there was a pool of sufficient size to divide into tranches and sell.

Also, once the market was established, mid-tier banks such as St George, Suncorp and Macquarie became aggressive users of securitisation for their own mortgages. So did foreign-owned banks such as BankWest and ING. Securitisation enabled the mid-tier banks and the non-bank lenders to occupy 30 per cent of the outstanding mortgage market by 2006. The 'big four' banks—ANZ, Westpac, NAB and CBA—were down to 60 per cent market share. The remaining 10 per cent was made up of marginal players such as building societies and credit unions.

The big four also used securitisation to a degree. The total RMBS market grew 3800 per cent from under A$5.4 billion in 1995 to above A$204 billion in mid

2007.[26] Initially, most of these securities were sold to local investors. But as the boom gathered pace and the local market became saturated, they were increasingly issued to offshore investors. At the end of 1995, 11 per cent of securities issued were to international buyers. By 1999 the figure had grown to 34 per cent. In December 2004 it had jumped to 43 per cent.[27]

And what of the troublesome residual tranches of high-risk securities that ultimately proved so disastrous to US shadow banking? The repackaging of residual tranches as CDOs did not happen in any volume in the lead-up to the Great Crash. Although the Australian CDO market was growing fast, from well under A\$500 million in 2001 to A\$15 billion in 2007, it was dominated by underlying corporate loans and associated synthetic tranches.[28]

According to one industry source, the Australian market was not big enough to make the securitisation of tranches viable. The role of the LMIs in providing credit enhancement meant that residual tranches were much smaller in Australian securitisations. Most residual tranches represented under 3 per cent of the overall pool, and 'to hire a team of pros to create exotic securities would have been exceedingly expensive'.

There was also a structural difference in the Australian process in that those who wrote the mortgages often retained the residual tranche or some stake in the mortgage pool. Thus the originator received revenue over time, through the cash flow generated by the mortgages, rather than exclusively through up-front fees as in the US. The former head of global securitisation at Société Générale and current Australian Securities and

Investments Commissioner, Greg Medcraft, maintains, 'that this "skin in the game" helped keep Australian brokers from the excessive abuses of underwriting standards apparent in the US'.

However, as we have seen, the US investment banks that owned mortgage brokers also had 'skin in the game' in the retained residual tranches that would prove to be their downfall. The investment bank, Merrill Lynch, controlled the large national originator, OwnIt. Yet some of OwnIt's securities had amongst the highest default rates recorded in the Crash, above 60 per cent.[29]

The investment mania fundamentally altered notions of prudence in the lender as much as it did the borrower.

The Long Shadow

The growing asset boom and falling savings rates meant that ANZ, NAB, CBA and Westpac found that the demand for loans outstripped deposits. Australian banks' ratio of deposits to total liabilities was 59 per cent in December 1994. By 2000 the ratio had dropped to 46 per cent. It finally hit 43 per cent in late 2007.[30]

Competition for loans with the new shadow bank sector was also intense, which gave rise to the big four's own shadow banking activities. They were cautious about securitisation, but their high (AA) ratings provided them with a different method for accessing funds to lend: the issue of bonds directly to international investors. The banks' foreign wholesale borrowings grew from A$30 billion in 1990 to A$100 billion in 2000. From there the borrowing escalated, reaching A$357 billion in

2008.[31] The Australian housing and consumption boom of the early twenty-first century was funded by foreign borrowing by the banks on a scale far greater than had ever happened before.[32]

Traditionally, banks had been cautious about this method of raising funds because it carried the added risks of managing currency and foreign interest-rate fluctuations. Consequently, according to Philip Bayley, former director of Capital Markets at Standard & Poor's Australia, 'there was a direct correlation between the big four's steady mastery of currency and interest rate swap derivatives and the rise of their borrowing in international wholesale markets'. These shadow instruments grew even more rapidly than the underlying borrowing. In 1990, Australian bank books showed a combined total of A$1.57 trillion notional derivative exposure. By 2000, the notional figure had grown to A$3.59 trillion, and in 2007 shot above A$13 trillion.[33]

As the boom hit new heights in 2004, there were other signs that Australia's big banks were becoming more comfortable with complex shadow banking activities. NAB, for example, launched an A$18 billion SIV that used short-term debt from money markets to buy high-yield, high-rated (but actually highly risky) securities such as CDOs and repackage them for investors. The spread between the short-term debt interest rate and the long-term securities was NAB's profit. But when the money markets that supplied the short-term debt froze in September 2007, the SIV was unable to roll over its debt and the rapidly devaluing securities had to be accounted for on the bank's balance sheets. As of May 2009, NAB financial disclosures showed that it had not written down the securities, despite their market value dropping A\$4 billion.[34]

The growing use of shadow bank methods fuelled a decade-long golden age of profits that culminated in a surge of earnings after the turn of the millennium. The growth of the banks and the intensification in the use of their capital is clear in their assets. In 1990, Australian banks held A\$326 billion in assets. It took nine years to double these to A\$669 billion. But in the next four years the assets grew another 59 per cent to A\$1.06 trillion. From 2003 to 2008 the assets nearly doubled again to A\$2.06 trillion.[35] We can add to this the growth in assets held or issued by those creating securities from A\$141 billion in December 2003 to a peak of A\$274 billion in June 2007. Increased shadow banking activities supercharged financial sector growth and credit supply in Australia.

The dramatic growth of non-bank lenders' activities and the banks' growing ease with shadow banking methods suggest that a transformation to US-style shadow banking was underway. Had there not been a Great Crash, intense competition in the mortgage market may have led Australian financial firms to offer mortgage products more easily to borrowers with substandard credit records.

As it was, unlike in the United States, the Australian house ownership rate did not change through the early twenty-first century. A delayed wave of innovative loans may well have changed that. Ian Rogers, editor of *The Sheet*, the Australian bank newsletter, says that 'the major difference between Australia and the US is that we were four years behind'.

Nonetheless, the metamorphosis was advanced enough that when the crisis began in late 2007, the Australian shadow bank sector was confronted with insolvency. When the crisis hit its peak in late 2008, the traditional banks faced the same fate. Risk within individual institutions may have been well managed, but it was replaced with the rampant systemic risk of a run by foreign investors.

The Heart of Darkness

One quadrillion dollars is a lot of money. That's one thousand million million, and it's the total notional value of derivative products issued since the millennium by financial intermediaries around the world.[36]

If shadow banking is a system that existed beyond the scrutiny of regulators, used clever risk-shifting instead of capital reserves to manage volatility, and intermediated investor savings rather than deposit savings, then it is reasonable to define the derivatives that made this possible as shadow instruments.

According to the Bank of International Settlements (BIS), as of June 2008, the total notional outstanding value of over-the-counter (OTC) derivatives stood at $683.7 trillion.[37] Just what purpose did these extraordinary quantities of derivatives serve, beyond the generation of extraordinary incomes for those who manufactured and sold them? The magnitude and youth of these products leads to the unsettling answer that nobody knows.

As former New York Federal Reserve President Gerald Corrigan told policymakers and financiers in

May of 2007: 'Anyone who thinks they understand this stuff is living in la-la land'.[38]

Some products, such as the credit default swap (CDS), aimed to shift risk from one company to another. A CDS is an insurance policy on the debt of another company. In a way, it is no more complex than a parent being the guarantor on his or her child's mortgage. On the other hand, with CDS the exchange is between two companies and one is paying the other for the service. In our example, if the bank were paying a fee to the parent to guarantee the child's loan, then a CDS would have been written by the parent for the bank; that is, the parent is being paid to absorb the default risk of the child's loan.

In theory, this means that companies can manage their risk with greater subtlety and spread it among many other companies. This was the rationale offered by those who embraced the use of shadow instruments over the past decade. In 2003, Alan Greenspan told a Senate banking committee:

> What we have found over the years in the market-place is that derivatives have been an extra-ordinarily useful vehicle to transfer risk from those who shouldn't be taking it to those who are willing and are capable of doing so.[39]

However, in practice, most obviously in the financial sector, this often means that companies feel they have offset the risk and have no need to keep capital in reserve against something going wrong. They are encouraged to take greater risks.

Moreover, because CDS are over-the-counter (OTC) derivatives, they need be known only by the two parties to the transaction. They are hidden from regulators, investors and everybody else. During the Crash of 2008, when confidence was tested, the risk that had been shifted from thousands of individual companies suddenly became a risk to the entire system. Because nobody knew where the risk lay, everyone was suspect.

The CDS shifts risk, but does not eliminate it. It is only as effective in shifting risk as the counterparty that wrote the guarantee is creditworthy. If the insuring counterparty fails, then the insured company is suddenly overexposed. This can lead to a chain reaction of failure, precisely the type of domino effect that US authorities neutralised when they bailed out AIG.

Two other major criticisms are made of the CDS. The first is that it provides incentives to some traders to bankrupt the company against which the CDS is written. If the lenders of the original debt are insured with a CDS, they can derail any negotiation to save troubled but viable firms because they have more to gain from bankruptcy. In early 2009, the *Financial Times* described several cases in which electronic finance threatened to trump the real economy.[40]

Second, a CDS enables an investor to bet against the health of a company's debt. Those in favour argue that it helps with 'price discovery', determining the correct value for companies' equity, bonds and other securities. The case against is argued by Satyajit Das, author of *Traders, Guns & Money: Knowns and Unknowns in the Dazzling World of Derivatives*:

CDS contracts did, in all probability, amplify losses in the credit market in recent defaults. For example, when Lehman Brothers defaulted, the firm had around $600 billion in debt. This would have been the maximum loss to creditors in the case of default. According to market estimates, there were CDS contracts of around $400 billion to $500 billion where Lehman was the reference entity ... If used for hedging, the CDS contracts would merely have resulted in the losses to creditors being transferred to the sellers of protection, leaving the total loss unchanged. Market estimates suggest that only around $150 billion of the CDS contracts were hedges. The remaining $250 billion to $350 billion of CDS contracts were not hedging underlying debt. The losses on these CDS contracts (in excess of $200 billion to $300 billion) are in addition to the $600 billion.[41]

The BIS records the rise of CDS globally, from the outstanding notional amount of $6.4 trillion in 2004 to $57.9 trillion at the conclusion of 2007.[42]

Two other forms of derivative, interest rate and currency contracts, grew at a similarly astonishing pace. At the conclusion of 2007, interest rate forwards, swaps and options made up 67 per cent of the notional value of global outstanding derivatives at $458.3 trillion. Currency forwards, swaps and options comprised the second largest category at $62.9 trillion.[43] In general, when these interest rate and currency contracts are combined into a package they enable companies to trade a floating rate of interest for a fixed rate of interest or vice-versa on an asset or liability, allowing a bank or company to hedge the risk of borrowing in a foreign market.

Let's say an Australian bank issues a bond in Japan. The bond is a five-year loan and is in Japanese yen. The bank has agreed to pay the bond holder interest every month and return the principal at the maturity date in yen. The bank is therefore exposed to two risks. One is the possibility that the Australian dollar will fall against the yen, making it more expensive to repay the interest and principal. The second is the possibility that interest rates rise in Japan, again making interest payments more expensive.

At the same time, another bank, firm or hedge fund has borrowed the same amount in Australian dollars and invested them in Japanese property. They are exposed to the same two risks in reverse. The two firms agree to swap the cash flows from their two loans. Each is now operating within the local currency and interest rates. They are both hedged.

In this example, our counterparties' needs match precisely. But in the real world, things are not so simple. There are times when there is more demand for swapping into Australian currency than there is to swap out of it. This means that those offering to swap with our Australian bank do not have a fully matching need for yen. To go ahead with the transaction they are therefore assuming some of the risk of the bank's borrowing, for which they charge a premium. The greater the amount of risk a counterparty takes on, the greater the speculative dimension of the swap and the greater the risk premium and potential loss. Of course, the counterparty can then hedge its transaction with another counterparty. But at some point, if the Australian dollar falls, the counterparty at the end of the chain carries the risk.

Global capital markets are made up of banks, shadow banks, hedge funds, insurance companies, pension funds and myriad investors playing this shadow game of hedge and counter-hedge. Each looks to find a profit margin by managing the risks surrounding the passage of enormous quantities of money across different markets, assets and currencies. The process of profiting from price mismatches in these markets is called arbitrage.

The BIS recorded the daily global turnover of traditional foreign exchange transactions in 2007 as just short of $3.2 trillion, up from $1.49 trillion in 1998.[44] Over the same period, daily global turnover of OTC foreign exchange and interest rate derivatives, those beyond exchanges and scrutiny, grew from $1.26 trillion to $4.2 trillion.[45] Global capital markets turn over foreign exchange and derivatives at the equivalent value of annual global GDP every seven days.[46] This is the core of the global shadow banking system.

There is no way to gauge how much of this activity is hedging or the financing of real commerce between companies in different nations, and how much of it is speculative. The only guide we have is the BIS *Triennial Foreign Exchange and Derivatives Market Survey for 2007*. It records that those trading traditional foreign exchange are divided into three categories: reporting dealers, which are banks and investment banks; non-reporting financial institutions, such as hedge funds, mutual funds, pension funds and insurance companies; and non-financial customers. The BIS says that the last category, comprising 17 per cent of the $3.8 trillion daily turnover of traditional foreign exchange, is 'likely to be related to … international trade in goods and services'. However, the category also includes government trans-actions. If so, then the remainder is either financial or speculative in nature.[47]

A similar pattern is apparent in the OTC currency derivatives market, where non-financial customers make up 27 per cent of the $2.32 trillion daily turnover. In the OTC interest rate derivatives market, non-financial customers were involved in less than 10 per cent of the $1.68 trillion daily turnover.[48]

The BIS categories show how the traditional bank versus shadow banking divisions that were defined by the national regulation of financial services for much of the twentieth century have become meaningless within the derivatives trade of global capital markets. For instance, in the United States, the top three derivative dealers have been the deposit-taking banks JPMorgan, Bank of America and Citibank; fourth was the investment bank Goldman Sachs.[49] In Australia, the four major deposit-taking banks are active across all derivative categories, just as are the Australian offices of the many international investment banks.[50]

The trading of shadow instruments enabled banks to grow beyond the constraints of their domestic economy. The banks no longer needed to worry about a local funding base of savings. Instead, they could channel offshore savings into lending and asset price appreciation in their home market. These offshore borrowings were and remain beyond the support of the central bank and its national lender-of-last-resort system. Put another way, shadow instruments may be able to manage currency and interest rate risk, but they do nothing about the liquidity risk inherent in a change of global investor sentiment. In this sense, all banks that participate in the global trade of shadow instruments are shadow banks.

The global shadow banking system is as intricate, swift and beautiful as the chemical transmissions within a living organism. It is the circulatory system of global capitalism. It exists beyond the understanding and control of any regulator or nation. The system can inundate chosen assets, markets, even countries with capital, or starve them on a whim. It can transmit shocks around the globe in an instant. It is the lifeblood of the Great Crash elephant.

5

Greed

IN OCTOBER 2007, during a New York conference dedicated to financial regulation, a respected Wall Street gentleman, powerbroker and sometime regulator spoke eloquently about contemporary US guidelines. Relaxed and comfortable in a lounge chair, silver hair swept back from his forehead, he held forth: 'Chinese walls are required to be established at brokerage firms ... it doesn't mean there aren't abuses for sure. But, by and large in today's regulatory environment, it's virtually impossible to violate rules'.[1]

The speaker was the ice-cool Bernard Madoff, the founder and chairman of a Wall Street market-making firm, and former chairman of the NASDAQ, one of New York's two stock exchanges. Madoff's firm had a blue-chip clientele that included such household names as Steven Spielberg, John Malkovich and Larry King, as well as a who's who of leading global banks.

A little over a year later, Madoff was charged with the largest fraud in the history of homo sapiens. At the time of his arrest, he had accumulated more than $60 billion of client assets but had dispersed 99.99 per cent of them, leaving only $50 million for investors to collect. As of June 2009, the agents of the law had found $1 billion or so of the missing assets, and were still looking for more.

Madoff had operated a Ponzi scheme, which takes its name from the 1920s swindler Charles Ponzi. The scam invented by Ponzi was described by John Kenneth Galbraith in his book *The Great Crash of 1929* as a prime exhibit for the greed and excess that laid the path to the Great Depression. It offers high returns to early investors, who are paid out of subscriptions by new investors. The operator of the scheme skims off some of the investors' money on the way through. The system can keep going for as long as subscriptions keep expanding. As soon as they don't, it collapses.

The losses of the original Ponzi scheme now look modest. The 1920s investors lost what in today's currency would be a fraction of 1 per cent of the money tied up in the Madoff scam. How could one man work a fraud of this scale? Because a vast network of managers channelled money to Madoff from across the world. They passed him billions of dollars, and he delivered regular returns—for a time.

Following Madoff's confession and conviction, US federal regulators warned of a 'rampant Ponzimonium' as they disclosed investigations into 'hundreds' of possible scams. A commissioner at the Commodities Futures Trading Commission said the watchdog was 'seeing more of these scams than ever before'.[2] This should not have come as a surprise. Amitai Aviram showed in the *Yale Journal on Regulation* that Ponzi investigations are a clear countercyclical signal, dropping off in the good times and booming in the bad.[3]

Economics Professor Hyman Minsky of Washington University, St Louis was made famous by his insight that long and stable booms in capitalist economies result in increasing Ponzi activity. Minsky describes the place of Ponzi arrangements in the three risk categories of financing in a boom:

> Hedge financing units are those which can fulfill all of their contractual payment obligations by their cash flows ... speculative finance units are units that can meet their payment commitments on 'income account' on their liabilities, even as they cannot repay the principal out of income cash flows. Such units need to 'roll over' their liabilities or issue new debt to meet commitments on maturing debt ... Ponzi finance units are those whose cash flows from operations are not sufficient to fill either the repayment of principal or the interest on outstanding debts by their cash flows from operations. Such units can sell assets or borrow. Borrowing to pay interest or selling assets to pay interest (and even dividends) on common stocks lowers the equity of a unit, even as it increases liabilities and the prior commitment of future incomes.[4]

Minsky's description goes beyond scoundrels such as Bernard Madoff. It defines many of the high-leverage strategies of the day. Madoff knew that his investors would lose their money one day, just as others would have known that their investors would almost certainly lose theirs.

It may seem glib to point the finger at Greed as a cause of the Great Crash. Greed is an eternal element in human behaviour, one of the seven deadly sins, and a component of all bubbles and manias. However, this particular boom and bust was driven in part by changes to the constraints placed on individuals in positions of responsibility in the financial markets, who in turn enhanced their own or others' incomes through actions that created great risks for the institutions to which they had a duty of care.

Here we look at regulatory capture, executive remuneration and fraud in the lead-up to the Crash. Changes in behaviour in these areas were systematic and institutionalised, and were vital in pushing the shadow banking boom to precarious heights.

Regulatory Capture

The economist George Stigler of the Chicago School of Economics defined a process called 'regulatory capture', in which those who guard the rules governing an industry succumb to the views of those whom they regulate. An illustration of Stigler's hypothesis transpired between Wall Street banks and US officials from the mid 1980s. As the complexity and sophistication of US financial markets grew, an increasing number of senior bankers

and officials crossed the porous boundary between Wall
Street, the Federal Reserve and the Treasury. These
individuals had a profound effect on policy.

The first man to make the move, and the most influential in the creation of shadow banking, was the Wall
Street insider and former non-executive director of
JPMorgan Bank, Alan Greenspan. Greenspan's appointment as chairman of the US Federal Reserve in 1987
came on the heels of a revolutionary vote by its board to
allow traditional banks to produce 5 per cent of their revenues from investment banking activities such as securities underwriting. The change was voted through despite
the objections of the then chairman, Paul Volcker, who
expressed a fear that lenders would recklessly lower loan
standards in pursuit of lucrative securities offerings, and
would market bad loans to the public.[5]

As history now records, Volcker's vision came to
fruition. But that did not impair Greenspan's faith in self-
regulating, self-correcting financial markets. According
to the *Wall Street Journal*, even as unease about mortgage fraud grew among some Federal Reserve governors
around 2000, Greenspan prevented action. This extended
to proposals by Edward Gramlich, Federal Reserve governor from 1997 to 2005, to use the Reserve's discretionary
authority to crack down on predatory lending. Even in
late 2004, when enthusiasm for the US housing bubble
reached fever pitch, Greenspan found a favourable
interpretation for events, remarking that 'improvements
in lending practices driven by information technology
have enabled lenders to reach out to households with
previously unrecognized borrowing capacities'.[6]

Greenspan's appointment was the first in a series of top Washington economic policy positions given to Wall Street titans. In January 1993 Robert Rubin ended twenty-six years at Goldman Sachs, latterly as chairman, to enter Clinton's White House as assistant to the president for economic policy, becoming Treasury secretary two years later. Rubin remained secretary until July 1999, when his deputy, Larry Summers, took over for the remainder of Clinton's final term. Ruben's public service is widely and rightly regarded as a high point in the management of some aspects of US public finances. His role in the securing of a strong budget position for the US was important to the prosperity of the 1990s.

However, this reputation sits sadly alongside his subsequent career. A few months after Rubin's resignation from the Treasury, the Glass-Steagall Act was finally repealed under intense pressure from a proposed merger of the insurance firm Travelers and the commercial bank Citicorp.[7] Within days of the announcement, Rubin joined the newly merged Citigroup as director, senior counsellor and, briefly, chairman. Citigroup then pursued a high-leverage strategy that included expansion into many of the areas that would unravel in the Great Crash. Rubin departed the bank in January 2009 when it was on government life-support. He had been paid $126 million for his service in the era of Clever Money.[8]

Rubin was said to have been 'joined at the hip to Greenspan' in the successful struggle to resist the regulation of shadow banking.[9] The two men oversaw several other legislative shifts that encouraged the development of shadow banking, and generally resisted efforts to regulate its new derivative instruments. In 1997 and 1998, when the then chairman of the Commodity and Futures Trading Commission, Brooksley Born, sought oversight of the burgeoning over-the-counter derivatives market, she was defeated by the combined power of the two men. In 2000, the Commodities Futures Modernization Act freed derivatives from regulatory scrutiny altogether.

Institutional faith in market self-regulation also played its part in the early 2002 decision by the Federal Reserve, the Federal Deposit Insurance Corporation (FDIC) and Treasury to alter the rules governing the supervision of securitisation by the credit rating agencies. Banks were suddenly freed from having to keep capital in reserve against the risk in low-rated securitisation tranches. In 2008, FDIC Chairman Sheila Bair, looking back at the 2002 change, conceded that:

> It may not be entirely coincidental that, in the subsequent years, financial service companies swung into high gear creating new classes of rated securities. These products were very attractive to banks that wanted to boost returns on equity, and to economize on regulatory capital ... In retrospect, regulators may have unintentionally encouraged banks to bet heavily on a new class of non-transparent securities.[10]

Regulatory rollback continued in 2004 when, under the guidance of Basel II, the Securities and Exchange Commission allowed the big five Wall Street investment banks to raise their leverage ratios from 12-to-1 to

35-to-1 or more. Just three years later, three of the five ceased to exist because of debt-charged collapses.

Tragedy became farce when, also in 2004, the Federal Bureau of Investigation (FBI) publicly warned of an epidemic of mortgage fraud. The warning included a prediction that if it was allowed to continue, the fraud would cause a crisis at least as large as the savings and loan (S&L) debacle, which had cost the US taxpayer around $150 billion. According to William Black, a regulator during the S&L crisis, 500 white-collar specialists within the FBI had been transferred to terrorism units following the September 11 attacks and had not been replaced, despite the warning. Lacking the manpower to pursue an investigation, the FBI formed an alliance with the Mortgage Bankers Association, the peak body for the mortgage originators, and instead produced a poster that warned against fraud.[11]

Mark Twain once said that history doesn't repeat itself, but it sure does rhyme. It rhymed in 2006 when Henry (Hank) Paulson, another Goldman Sachs chairman, was appointed Treasury secretary under George W Bush. The murky boundaries that are a hallmark of regulatory capture were apparent again two years later when the bailout of American Insurance Group (AIG) channelled almost $13 billion to Goldman Sachs. Other Goldman Sachs alumni who were central to the AIG bailout included Edward Liddy, who was appointed the company's new CEO, and Neel Kashkari, Paulson's deputy with responsibility for overseeing at least part of the bailout funds.[12]

The certainty of regulators and officials that a new age of banking perfection had begun was apparent in the

suspension of FDIC insurance premiums for banks. The
FDIC is responsible for insuring deposits and examining
and supervising financial institutions, as well as managing
receiverships. It does so using funds accumulated from
the premiums, but between 1996 and 2006 none were
collected. When Barney Frank, chairman of the House
Financial Services Committee, was asked why this was so,
he replied, 'We had this period where we had no failures …
The banks were saying, "Don't charge us anything"'.[13]

The legislative shifts and murky boundaries were
supported by the third pillar of regulatory capture: a
money politics machine of staggering proportions. For
instance, from 1990 to 2008, the finance, insurance and
real estate sectors contributed more than $2.2 billion
dollars to political parties and staff. The same group
spent another $3.4 billion on lobbying between 1998
and 2008. Expenditure of this kind by the financial
services sector grew an average 10 per cent per annum
throughout the golden period of banking. This suggests
that companies were enjoying a satisfactory return on
investment in the political process.[14]

In 2009, Simon Jonson, former chief economist of
the International Monetary Fund and Professor of Entre-
preneurship at Massachusetts Institute of Technology's
Sloan School of Management, openly compared this
confluence of regulators and bankers with the corruption
endemic in developing countries during past financial
crises:

The U.S. economic and financial crisis is shockingly
reminiscent of moments we have recently seen in

emerging markets (and only in emerging markets): South Korea (1997), Malaysia (1998), Russia and Argentina (time and again). But there's a deeper and more disturbing similarity: elite business interests—financiers, in the case of the U.S.— played a central role in creating the crisis, making ever-larger gambles, with the implicit backing of the government, until the inevitable collapse. More alarming, they are now using their influence to prevent precisely the sorts of reforms that are needed, and fast, to pull the economy out of its nosedive. The government seems helpless, or unwilling, to act against them.[15]

Executive Remuneration

Joe Cassano is the bespectacled, balding, 54-year-old New Yorker who is widely credited with destroying AIG. Cassano headed AIG's Financial Products Unit based in Mayfair, London. He had been with the firm since its inception in 1987, but it wasn't until 2000 that he ascended to the position of CEO. That was the year in which the US Congress passed the Commodity Futures Modernization Act, which freed global derivative trading.

That convergence saw Cassano orchestrate the creation of more than $80 billion worth of credit default swaps related to US subprime collateralised debt obligations within five years. In March 2008, after losses in the Financial Products Unit had pushed AIG to an

$11.5 billion quarterly loss, Cassano stepped down. He left the company having earned $280 million, and with a $1 million per month consulting contract.[16] In April 2009, he was under investigation by both US and English authorities.[17]

The rise and fall of Joe Cassano offers a useful parallel with contemporary finance for one more reason. The Financial Products Unit operated in a holding company that gave its executives 30 per cent of the profits from the operation. In addition, Financial Products booked its profits up-front, even though its parent firm had to carry the risk of the deals for years into the future. Half of the executive compensation arising from these profits was paid immediately and the other half over several years, depending upon the deals. This provided executives with enormous motivation to write as much business as they possibly could. By the time of the Great Crash, AIG was exposed to $500 billion in liabilities, enough to destroy the company and most of Wall Street with it.[18]

Cassano is symbolic of a plague that swept financial services during the boom: executives arbitraging their own companies for personal reward. The scale of remuneration packages in financial services was such that for at least some people, it pushed other motivations into the background. A few years of 'successes' could set up your family in material security, influence and prestige for generations to come. For some, this was worth risking other values and goals.

The emergence of shadow banking was accompanied by major changes in the amount and form of remuneration in the financial sector more generally.

In the early 1980s, Jack Welch, CEO of General Electric, promoted 'shareholder value' as the principle that should guide executive decision making. The interests of executives could be 'aligned' with those of shareholders if remuneration were linked to shareholder value. This was measured period by period, by the increase in the share price plus dividends paid. The latter was of relatively minor importance in a rising market.

The idea came to be applied by issuing bonus share rights or options. Remuneration came to be doubly leveraged to the share price: more rights and options were issued when the share price rose strongly, and the rights were worth more in those circumstances. The leverage was especially large in the case of options.

There was something to be said for the alignment of executive interests with shareholder interests. Only later did people observe that shareholders' value had generally increased at a reasonable rate in earlier times, and was destroyed in the period when executive remuneration was aligned most strongly with shareholder interests. To the extent that the share price was related to the performance of the firm rather than to the general market, it was closely related to short-term profitability. This brought the horizons of executive focus dramatically forward, generating a search for ways in which a higher proportion of the value created within a firm took the form of short-term profits. These could be traded off against long-term profits, and sometimes against increased risk to the stability and survival of the firm.

One way in which this was done was to extract the expected future profits from new business as a fee at the time of the transaction, rather than as a margin on a loan or other financial instrument over its life. The consequence was that it rewarded richly the writing of new business, and not at all the continued profitability of the loan or instrument beyond the point that an executive ceased to be responsible for it. The executive had received the bonus on the basis of the initial writing of the loan. It would not be taken back when the loan went bad.

Share options became increasingly distorted through the boom, not least because they rewarded executives for stock market rises that had nothing to do with the value that they had added to their companies. *Financial Times* journalist Francesco Guerrera wrote in March 2009 that 'in banking, end-of year awards of options and stock had the added drawback of remunerating staff well before the company or its shareholders could find out whether their bets had paid off'. In the same article, Jack Welch repudiated his own doctrine of shareholder value, describing it as 'a dumb idea'.[19]

Dumb or not, the focus on short-term profits and bonuses proved to be an unprecedented bonanza for Wall Street bankers and traders. In 1995 they earned a total of $8 billion in bonuses, and by 2006 this had increased to an extraordinary $37 billion. Even in 2008, after the crisis had generated large-scale nationalisations and bailouts, Wall Street's bonus pool remained at $18.4 billion.[20] In June the *Guardian* reported that Goldman Sachs and Morgan Stanley employees were on track for their highest ever bonuses for the 2009 year. Bank executives responded that it was too soon to say.[21]

Australian Echoes

In Australia, similar forces were introduced through the globalisation of the senior executive market. The appointment of four Americans as CEOs of major Australian companies in the early 1990s was particularly influential: Bob Joss at Westpac (1990), Frank Blount at Telstra (1992), George Trumble at AMP (1994) and Paul Anderson at BHP (1998).

These appointments were made at remuneration levels well above and in different forms to those paid to Australian executives at the time. Bob Joss's base salary when he was appointed was almost as high as the base salaries of the CEOs of the other three major banks combined.[22] In addition, his 'performance-related' remuneration components exceeded the base salary in value, while they were small for the Australian bank executives. By the time of Joss's departure five years later, the base salary in the other banks was similar to Joss's at the time of his appointment. In addition, at the later date, their performance-related payments exceeded the value of the base remuneration.[23]

These appointments were influential in the general structuring of remuneration packages in Australia. Alongside the increase in base salary, the performance-related component rose from 9.5 per cent of the total to almost half between 1987 and 2000.[24] The total value of remuneration packages increased several-fold between 2000 and 2007.

What difference did greater performance-related remuneration have on executive performance? That would require a major study in itself, and that study has not yet been done. We can observe that of the four seminal recruitments of Americans in the early 1990s, two (Joss and Anderson) transformed their companies as their boards would have hoped they would. Another underperformed in comparison to the general level of Australian CEOs, while the fourth performed less satisfactorily still.

The shifting of remuneration levels and structures towards American norms went furthest in the investment banks with large interests in asset management. The Australian leaders of the sector included Macquarie Bank, Babcock & Brown and Allco Finance. Babcock & Brown and Allco Finance in particular shared business models with similar characteristics to those that sank Wall Street: complex business structures, reliance on fee income from transactions, opaque accounting, and exorbitant remuneration biased towards reward for what was in reality short-term performance.

Babcock & Brown provides a stark example of the system's focus on short-term outcomes without regard for what happens next. In early 2008, it paid out roughly $600 million in bonuses for the previous year's work. Within twelve months the company was bankrupt, unable to pay roughly $600 million in debts immediately due. Its expected loss for the year was reported in June 2009 as being more than A$5.4 billion. The figures were revealed as its founding chairman was reported to be supervising the construction of a A$15 million house in San Francisco. Meanwhile, the former CEO was reported to be enduring a northern hemisphere summer split between Tuscany, Wimbledon and the Ashes cricket test at Lords.[25]

Penalties for Criminal Behaviour

The appropriate punishment for clear breaches of the laws of finance should be the simplest of regulatory matters. However, the law enforcement systems and agencies have had difficulties in matching the punishment to the crime. Temptations are introduced by the combination of huge rewards for short-term business performance, society's respect for those who remain rich after conviction for white-collar crimes, the opportunity to buy a reputation in a modern market economy, and relatively light penalties for those found guilty. They leave an ambiguous balance of incentives for people who are not strongly motivated by internal moral constraints.

People in financial markets who were weighing up the risks of criminal behaviour in the boom before the Crash had only history to guide them. Experience told them that the chances of detection were not high, and those of conviction were lower still. Those who attempted to calculate the costs should they be convicted of financial crime might also have taken some comfort from history.

Michael Milken was the leading figure at Drexel Burnham Lambert, and the inventor and facilitator of the 'junk bond' in the 1980s. Junk bonds were issued by high-risk companies and paid a high interest rate in recognition of that risk. Milken and his company were active in selling the bonds to savings and loan societies and other institutions that were unfamiliar with sophisticated finance. The company was said to have misrepresented the risk to borrowers, and Milken was found by the courts to be guilty of serious breaches of the law.

This was all part of the S&L scandal of the 1980s, unleashed by an early Reagan-era round of badly designed financial deregulation. Milken served twenty-two months of a 10-year gaol sentence—it has been said, in comfortable circumstances. Today he is known mainly and favourably for his charitable activities. *Fortune* magazine estimated his net worth in 2007 at US$2.1 billion.[26]

We might offer the last word on Greed to Rodney Adler, perhaps Australia's most notorious convicted white-collar criminal. Adler was a key player in the collapse of HIH Insurance, Australia's largest corporate bankruptcy. In an interview with David James at *BRW* magazine in May 2009, Adler said:

> There has been a major change in the upper middle-management layer of most corporations. In the old days, which certainly I believe in, the standard organisation was that equity went into a company, and if you owned that equity after 20 years' hard work you made a lot of money if you were successful.
>
> About 10 or 20 years ago this all changed. All of a sudden these people on good salaries who hadn't taken the risk, who hadn't built the corporation, they said to themselves: 'I'd like to be rich. I'd like to have equity in the company but

I don't want to buy it.' And a whole new set of instruments evolved out of America, which then infested the rest of the world, certainly the Western world, where executives became owners but with no risk.

[At that point] capitalism as we know it changed. It is not capitalism because the risk has gone. The executives have the upside and no downside. That is the problem.[27]

Part II
Bust

6

Things Fall Apart

THE US FEDERAL RESERVE records the first salient date of the Great Crash as 7 February 2007: the day that the government-sponsored enterprise (GSE) Freddie Mac declared it would no longer buy subprime mortgages from mortgage originators.[1] But Freddie Mac's actions were clearly responding to something, and digging a little deeper pushes the time line back.

Nine months earlier, a US mortgage originator called Merit Financial had gone bankrupt. It had done so as the refinancing boom brought about by low interest rates in the post-2001 period came to an end. A subsequent investigation revealed the unorthodox lending practices that would come to characterise the Crash.

Merit was founded in 2001 by former Washington Huskies football star Scott Greenlaw, then aged twenty-nine. It specialised in lending to clients with a bad credit history (subprime borrowers). Within five years it had written more than $2 billion of mortgages and employed 400 people. According to the *Seattle Times*, Greenlaw employed loan officers in his own image. Many were ex-footballers, one an ex-Hooters girl. The loan officers went through a 19-step training program lasting one hour. After the bankruptcy, one employee confessed that many officers 'didn't even know how to read a credit report'.

Many former employees described Merit's working environment as a raucous, sometimes lewd 'frat party'. Merit provided kegs of beer for staff meetings, and employees were free to bring in six-packs on Fridays. Several loan officers boasted online that doing drugs was a favourite pastime. 'Let's get hopped up and make some bad decisions', wrote one beside a photo of himself grinning broadly.[2]

The end of Merit Financial is an appropriate inflection point for the beginning of the Great Crash.

Any of the four parts of the Great Crash elephant might have precipitated the crisis. China's boom and its imbalances may have been undone by a change of macro-economic strategy in either a deficit or a surplus country, perhaps in response to some bump in the road of economic growth. Western consumers may have reached some tipping point in their capacity to service debt. The animal spirits that had driven the boom may have turned around in panic. The greed of corporate and government figures may have crushed political support for the new financial system.

In the end, higher interest rates in response to inflation concerns triggered asset deflation and the circulatory system of the boom failed. The shadow banking system that transferred capital across the world, supported the imbalances, fed the booms and rewarded the greed, went into cardiac arrest.

Between the collapse of Merit Financial and the Freddie Mac announcement, another twenty-nine mortgage originators declared bankruptcy. These included the eleventh largest in the country, Merrill Lynch's OwnIt.[3] As the mortgage originators went bust, declines in house prices began to register on the Case-Shiller Home Price Index in July 2006. Seven months later, as Freddie Mac made its declaration, the index was down 3 per cent to 201 points.

Ben Bernanke, Chairman of the Federal Reserve Bank, and Secretary of the Treasury Hank Paulson both responded with reassuring comments about how mortgage problems were 'contained' in the subprime market. These comments were echoed by the investment banks Bear Stearns and Lehman Brothers.[4] The US stock market took comfort and, as measured by the Standard & Poor's 500 (S&P 500), blithely rallied towards its peak in October 2007.

But beneath the bullish rhetoric and bourse, the number of mortgage originator failures had continued, reaching fifty-one in March 2007. Sentiment took a heavy blow on 2 April when New Century Financial, the second largest originator of subprime mortgages for 2006, was liquidated. Two months later, the toll of mortgage originator bankruptcies had reached eighty-one and the Home Price Index had fallen steadily to 199, now down 4 per cent from its peak. On 1 June, the rating agencies

Moody's and Standard & Poor's broke from the closed
loop of securitisation and downgraded the AAA ratings
on a range of outstanding mortgage-backed securities
(MBS) and collateralised debt obligations. This was
immediately followed by the suspension of redemptions
at two highly geared Bear Stearns hedge funds that traded
the securities.

By late July, Bear Stearns was liquidating the two hedge
funds. Standard & Poor's placed another 612 securities
backed by subprime mortgages on credit watch, and
mortgage originator implosions reached 106. Bernanke
and Paulson repeated their assertion that the problem
was contained, and interest rates remained on hold.

In early August, the collapse of the market for asset-
backed securities (ABS) crossed the Atlantic when French
banking giant BNP Paribas halted redemptions at three
specialist ABS investment funds. In a press release, the
company explained: 'The complete evaporation of liquidity in certain market segments of the US securitisation
market has made it impossible to value certain assets
fairly regardless of their quality or credit rating'. In short,
conditions were deteriorating so fast that they couldn't
attribute any particular value to the assets.[5] This was the
turning point. Henceforth, the shadow banking system
ceased lending to and investing in ABS.

It didn't take long for the supply of capital to dry up.
By mid September the Bank of England had announced
plans to provide extraordinary loans to support Northern
Rock, the United Kingdom's fifth largest mortgage lender
and its most aggressive securitising bank.[6] It borrowed
heavily from short-term money-market funds so it could

write more mortgages than its deposit base would have allowed, then securitised the mortgages. The money-market funds refused to roll over Northern Rock's loans. Various players in the shadow banking system were now turning on one another. The securitisation chain on which all had relied was decoupling at every link. Northern Rock's predicament sent shock waves through UK consumer markets. There was an old-fashioned run on the bank and it was nationalised within five months.

In Australia, the first casualties were the non-bank lenders. With the investment world in outright panic about exotic securities, the market for Australia's plain vanilla residential mortgage-backed securities evaporated. This plunged the listed non-bank lender RAMS into immediate crisis as it was unable to refinance more than A\$6 billion of debt in short-term corporate paper markets. By October 2007 the company was being dismembered. Westpac bought the brand and its branches for A\$140 million. Numerous other non-bank lenders either wound down operations or disappeared over subsequent months.[7]

By September 2007, US mortgage originator deaths had hit 149. The government authorities continued their rhetoric about the fallout from the collapses being contained, but their actions suggested otherwise. The Federal Reserve cut the federal funds target rate by a larger amount than had become usual—50 basis points— on 18 September. A month later, another twenty-two mortgage originators failed and the Home Price Index slide had dropped to 191, down about 8 per cent. Finally, even the US stock market's rose-coloured glasses began to fog. The S&P 500, the main broadly based index of stocks on the New York Stock Exchange, reached an intraday peak of 1565 on 19 October. By year-end it was down nearly 7 per cent.

The US stock market continued its fall through January and February of 2008. The Federal Reserve's interest rates also kept coming down, by 25 points in November 2007 and again in December, followed by emergency cuts of 125 points in January. Any pretence that the shadow banking system was in a controlled shake-out was now abandoned.

Another shadow banking domino fell in January as the rating agencies Fitch and Standard & Poor's threatened to downgrade one of the main monoline insurers: AMBAC Financial. Then in March, the growing strife reached the centre of the securitisation machine. In the middle of that month, Bear Stearns, the number one US investment bank dealer in MBS, suddenly found itself insolvent.[8] Bear Stearns had begun the year with $11 billion of equity supporting $395 billion in assets, which meant a leverage of more than 35 to 1. Such a highly leveraged balance sheet, consisting of many illiquid and potentially worthless assets, could be sustained only with investor and lender confidence. That confidence was now falling apart.

Nouriel Roubini, professor of economics at the Stern School of Business, New York University, described what was happening as a 'generalised run on the shadow financial system'.[9]

Bear Stearns was sold to JPMorgan for $1.2 billion, with help from the New York Federal Reserve. The meltdown sent a huge shock through the US housing market, shadow banking system and stock market. When March arrived, mortgage originator deaths had soared to 241 and the Home Price Index had entered free-fall, plummeting to 172. The S&P 500 hit a new low of 1276, down 18.5 per cent from the previous October. Wall Street was joined in its bear market by the UK Stock Exchange index, the FTSE, which had also sunk 16 per cent from its October peak. Most international stock markets now followed suit.

However, there was continued buoyancy in commodity markets. Demand growth remained strong and was expected to continue on the back of expansion in China and the other large developing countries. A number of specific supply and demand factors helped to boost most food prices to record levels. And since the prices for most commodities, including oil, other energies and metals, are mostly set in US dollars, they were boosted by the fall in the US dollar that accompanied the Federal Reserve's aggressive reductions in interest rates. The prices of oil, natural gas, coal, copper and grains all reached historic peaks in or around the middle of 2008. And so the stock markets of countries in which resource stocks were of major importance held up better than others, at least for a while.

With its high concentration of resources stocks, the Australian stock market was one of these. Although down from its October 2007 peak, the main Australian stock price index, the All Ordinaries, continued to hold up reasonably well through the northern hemisphere troubles, right up until mid May 2008. However, the relative sectoral strengths were revealing. The Financials Index had steadily slid from the October 2007 peak of around 7500 to a March 2009 low of around 2700. This represented a loss of value of almost two-thirds in Australian dollar terms. The fall was much greater in international currency, as the Australian dollar— along with the currencies of other resource exporting countries—fell by more than 30 per cent against the US dollar in a short period after commodity prices began to slide in July. The Materials Index for resources stocks continued to rally through to a May 2008 peak above 17000 points.

While April, May and June of 2008 seemed relatively uneventful, with stock markets tracking sideways or declining slowly, beneath the calm surface the carnage in the US housing market continued to build. By the end of June, the Home Price Index had slid to 167, now down more than 20 per cent from its peak, and mortgage originator failures had climbed to 262. And in July, history resumed its relentless course across the whole spectrum of financial activity.

The equity prices of the pioneers of securitisation, Fannie Mae and Freddie Mac, had been sliding well ahead of the general stock market for over a year. Now, both stocks entered a death spiral. Making matters worse, the drying up of capital supply to securitisation meant that international investors had abandoned GSE debt and MBS. Foreign purchases of both collapsed. The Chinese Government, a major creditor to the American GSEs, sent a sharp message that there would be major consequences for Chinese capital flows to the United

States if there were capital losses on debt that had been presumed to have government backing.[10]

The problem dogging the GSEs was the same as that dragging down the other players in the shadow banking system. Owing to the complexity at the heart of shadow banking risk management, investors were simply unable to clarify which companies' earnings were going to be hit by the losses arising from the housing crash. Sensibly enough, investors therefore abandoned all of the players at risk. Such is the vulnerability of a system based purely upon confidence, as had been clearly demonstrated in many previous bank runs, including in the Great Depression.

Soon there was nowhere to hide the weakening realities and sentiment. In July, the prices of oil and a range of other commodities reached their peaks. In August, global nervousness about the ongoing housing and shadow banking crash pushed commodity markets down sharply, and by the end of the month, oil was down almost 30 per cent from the July peak.

Then came September. Entering the month, the Home Price Index registered 161, mortgage originator fatalities stood at 275 and the S&P 500 was steady at 1282 points. On 7 September, Fannie Mae and Freddie Mac succumbed to investor revulsion and were placed into 'conservatorship' by the US Federal Reserve. This was in reality a nationalisation—a socialisation of immense losses. The management and boards of the two firms were dismissed, and the US Treasury was issued with 79.9 per cent of preferred shares and warrants, effectively wiping out shareholders.

Before anyone could draw breath, on 15 September the core of global shadow banking leapt over the flailing GSEs and into oblivion. On that day, two of the remaining four investment banks responsible for building and running the securitisation machine ceased to exist. The first was Merrill Lynch, whose symbol of the charging bull was familiar in markets all over the world. Merrill Lynch mustered a half-crazed stampede of its businesses into a waiting corral at the Bank of America, where the mob was rebranded for $50 billion.

The thundering herd at Lehman Brothers hurtled straight off a cliff. The Federal Reserve had found no institution large, bold and uninformed enough to take any risk at all on it. Lehman Brothers filed for Chapter 11 bankruptcy, which rapidly developed into outright liquidation. This was the largest bankruptcy in US history. It left $613 billion in ordinary debts, $155 billion in bond debt, and assets worth $639 billion. Lehman's was counterparty to more than 8000 firms through its derivatives book.[11]

The following day the knacker called upon the American Insurance Group, shadow banking's most audacious insurance firm. The Federal Reserve stepped in and announced an $85 billion extraordinary loan to the stricken enterprise. It would be bailed out another three times over the subsequent four months to the tune of $170 billion and ultimately be nationalised as well. Its ribald financial products arm was wound down precipitously.[12]

The carnage in the shadow banking system wrought over September now sliced through the major arteries of equity markets, company and mainstream bank lending. Lehman Brothers had lines of credit open to more than

100 hedge funds, many of which were highly leveraged players in the equity markets. Its sudden bankruptcy meant that all of these lines of credit were called in at once. Desperate to raise cash, the funds sold equities and pushed prices lower. Risk aversion surged across the spectrum of other banks.

It was a gargantuan margin call on global equities. By the end of September, the S&P 500 was down to 1106 points; by 20 November, it had been cut in half from its peak to 752 points. All of the world's bourses followed closely behind. Other markets tended to fall further than New York, the 'risky' emerging markets most of all.

The scepticism that had gripped investors for eighteen months now took hold of the banks themselves. They demanded huge premiums on business loans or refused to lend at all, either to one another or to other corporations. LIBOR, the interest rate at which banks in London lend to other banks, shot to levels that howled an unwillingness to pass capital to even the safest banks. The short-term corporate debt market shut down completely. Known as the commercial paper market, it is the key source of cash flow for the day-to-day operations of the world's largest businesses. Trade finance also collapsed, with no bank keen to accept letters of credit to support importers and exporters. After all, the risk with the foreign counterparty was unknown.

The collapse in trust that was consuming shadow banking had now swallowed the basic financial operations of the entire global economy.

In the United States, traditional deposit-taking banks now joined the mass slaughter of mortgage originators.

The first to the knife was Washington Mutual, the sixth largest bank in the country. Depositors withdrew $16.7 billion, 9 per cent of the total, in the week following the Lehman Brothers collapse. The company was seized by the Federal Deposit Insurance Corporation (FDIC) and sold to JPMorgan Chase for just $2 billion at the end of September.[13]

Next in line was Wachovia, the fourth largest national bank by assets. On the heels of the Washington Mutual seizure, Wachovia also suffered a run by depositors, including $5 billion in just one day.[14] After some controversy, it was taken over by Wells Fargo in early October for $15 billion.

After having seen no bank failures in 2005 or 2006, and only four in 2007, the FDIC was deluged with thirty-seven bank collapses from September 2008 to March 2009.

Contagion was now also rife among highly leveraged banks in Europe. The Benelux giant Fortis was partially nationalised on 28 September. By the end of October, the giant British bank HBOS had been sold to Lloyds TSB of London and the combined group was partially nationalised, with the UK Treasury holding a 43 per cent shareholding. Icelandic banks Glitnir, Landsbanki and Kaupthing were all under government or regulator control.

In Australia, there was a huge outflow of deposits from mid-tier banks to the big four. Cash logistics companies were overstretched in responding to requests to transfer physical currency. A spectacle unfolded in which two of the major banks anxiously pushed takeovers for shaky mid-tier banks even as their own problems in refinancing wholesale debt intensified. More heavily dependent on overseas wholesale funding than banks in any other country, their ability to fund their business dried up suddenly. The Commonwealth Bank acquired BankWest from the flailing HBOS on 8 October. Westpac pushed for competition regulator approval of its buyout of St George Bank. The major banks advised the government that their capacity to absorb shaky second-tier banks and to continue in business depended on a government guarantee.

With refinancing no longer possible, and as short-term debt repayments came due, a desperate rush to sell assets at distressed prices took hold of Australian-listed asset managers. By 2009 the two investment banks, Allco Finance and Babcock & Brown, were in receivership. Overall, the listed property and infrastructure managers' market capitalisation was down 64 per cent to $83 billion.[15]

These shifts in value were accompanied by massive dislocations in currency markets. Entire countries were now having their asset stock devalued at astonishing speed. Generalised risk aversion dramatically lifted the value of the US dollar as investors worldwide dashed to buy dollars to repay US dollar-denominated loans. Between July and November, the US dollar appreciated 17 per cent against a basket of currencies.[16]

The same risk aversion also reversed the yen carry trade. Hedge funds, banks, other corporations and Japanese investors who had borrowed money in Japan and then reinvested it in much higher yielding emerging market assets scrambled to dump the assets and return the money to its source. The yen soared. Emerging market and commodity currencies, including the Australian dollar, fell 30 per cent and more against the US dollar.

What began in May 2006 with the collapse of a US mortgage lender escalated over twnety-nine months into worldwide debt revulsion. After the long boom, the system was now in complete reverse. The asset bubbles that underpinned Western prosperity had burst. The wondrous machine of shadow banking that supported the global imbalances was still.

A testament to the underlying strength of Platinum Age growth was that no major economy was conscious of being in recession prior to the September 2008 quarter. Unemployment had crept higher but had remained a fringe issue. The shock of September changed all of that. The Great Crash elephant had turned rogue and trampled debt-sopped consumers. They lay flat and did not move.

7

Economic Collapse

ON 15 AUGUST 2008, Ethan Harris, chief economist at Lehman Brothers, launched his new book, which studied the operations of the US Federal Reserve under its new chairman, Ben Bernanke.[1] The book's synopsis asked a timely question: 'How will Bernanke build on Greenspan's success?' The answer arrived four weeks later when Lehman Brothers became a smoking crater in Wall Street. Bernanke and others had decided not to stamp out Lehman's fizzing fuse. This answer was obviously a surprise to Harris, and yet the rationale of his book had been his special insights into the policy workings of the chairman's mind.

The most surprising fact about recessions is that they always come as a surprise. Former Bank of England economist Christopher Dow demonstrated this for the twentieth century in his study of major recessions.[2] People everywhere were slow to realise that they were in a global recession, and slower still to appreciate its severity. The collapse of Lehman Brothers in September trumpeted the arrival of an extraordinary downturn.

Long after the event, in December 2008, America's National Bureau of Economic Research said that the United States had been in recession since the end of 2007, although the data show that American output did not start to decline until the first quarter of 2008.[3] Output in Japan and some European countries began to fall at the end of 2007, but too late to stop the total growth of output for the year being high by historical standards.

Platinum Age growth had continued through 2006 and 2007 as subprime and banking problems began to ooze into international consciousness. The 5.2 per cent growth in global output in 2007, measured in purchasing power in the usual manner of the International Monetary Fund (IMF), was high by any historical standards. The collective contribution of the developing countries was stronger than ever. Together, they grew by a stunning 8.3 per cent, led by China's 13 per cent and India's 9.3 per cent. Africa, the problem region of global development, did particularly well with 6.2 per cent.[4]

Before September 2008, global recession wasn't the first thing on the minds of communities or their leaders. The Reserve Bank of Australia raised interest rates in February and again in March because it saw inflation as the greatest problem facing the national economy, while the Chinese premier's work report to the National People's Congress in March spoke of the need to reduce growth and bring inflation back under control. When the Group of Eight heads of government met in Japan in July, high global energy and food prices were the centre of attention. Even in August, the Governor of the People's Bank of China told a meeting in Basel that fighting inflation was the main focus of monetary policy.

When the fact that most of the developed countries were in recession was finally noticed, it was expected to be an 'ordinary' recession. The extraordinary recession of the 1930s was far from most minds—until September 2008, when the Great Crash in the global financial system quickly became the Great Recession in world output and trade.

The normal funding of business stopped. It did not only stop in the countries whose home banks had taken Clever Money and Greed to giddying new heights; it stopped everywhere. New lending for business investment and housing halted across the globe. Exporters could not get their usual banks to honour the usual letters of credit from their usual customers. Credit facilities were withdrawn from the wobbly and from the sound, who then became wobbly. This disruption to credit and an apprehension of risk reduced consumer spending and business investment everywhere. The sudden and large reduction in expenditure in the West, led by the Anglosphere, caused inventories to rise and imports to fall.

In China, factories began to receive emails from overseas customers cancelling orders. Stocks of cars and refrigerators and shoes and buttons overflowed from the warehouses and factory parking lots. Output from the world's biggest steel industry after years of explosive growth was 12.4 per cent lower in November 2008 than in the same month a year before.[5] Electricity output was more than 10 per cent lower. Goods stopped moving. Consumers everywhere made do with cheaper versions of familiar products. Factories in the richer economies that produced higher quality and more expensive goods— Japan, Korea and Taiwan—shut down faster than in China.

The International Monetary Fund's July 2008 forecasts looked to 3.9 per cent growth in global output for 2009, one-quarter lower than in what were then the recent years, a big downturn for the world. In December, the IMF revised its forecast down to 2.2 per cent. A new revision in January 2009 anticipated only 0.5 per cent, and within two months, heads of government preparing for the London Group of 20 meeting were told to expect growth in the range of 0.5 to minus 1.5 per cent. Output in advanced economies was expected to fall by 3.8 per cent, while low positive growth was anticipated in developing countries (1.6 per cent)—positive because of China and India.[6]

In July 2009 the estimate for 2009 had stabilised near the bottom of this range, at minus 1.4 per cent, with plus 1.5 per cent for emerging and developing economies.[7] Time will tell if the IMF estimate was too low for China, India and Indonesia, and therefore for developing countries as a whole.

Commodity Crash

Commodity prices fell rapidly from record highs. In June 2008, oil was at its highest price ever in real terms: nearly

US$150 per barrel in current dollars. By December it had fallen by two-thirds. Even so, it remained well above the levels of earlier recessions, and even than in most earlier periods of prosperity, but 69 per cent below its mid-year heights (see Figure 7.1). Copper fell from 350 cents to 130 cents per pound between June and December. Again, even after the 60 per cent fall, the price was high by the standards of earlier recessions (see Figure 7.2).

The persistence of reasonably high commodity prices after these large falls tells us that the tightness in global commodity markets during the early Platinum Age reflected long-term changes in the global balance between supply and demand.

Resource companies all over the world faced acute financing problems. The Australian base metals producer Oz Minerals was, like its bankers, unable to roll over its

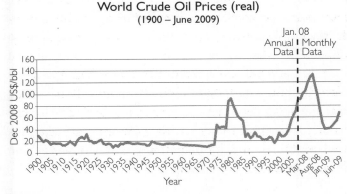

Figure 7.1

US CPI data: http://research.stlouisfed.org/publications/review/98/09/9809dw.dat & US Bureau of Labour Statistics
World Crude Oil Prices: Albert Clo (2000) 'Oil Economics and Policy' Springer, ISBN 0792379063 & US Energy Information Association (EIA)

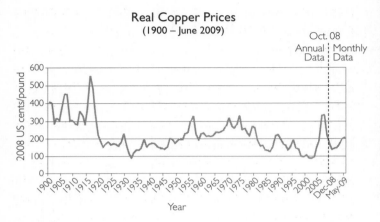

Figure 7.2

Copper prices: US Geological Survey (US Copper prices), International Copper Study Group & LME (World Copper prices)
US CPI data: http://research.stlouisfed.org/publications/review/98/09/9809dw.dat
& US Bureau of Labour Statistics

debts in October 2008. It appeared to have sound assets, the value of which would comfortably exceed its liabilities once normal financial conditions returned. But there was no time to wait for this. And unlike its bankers, it had no recourse to a government guarantee. The banks insisted that the company sell assets at the most difficult of times to clear debt. After noisy Australian political discussion, and the Australian Government's exclusion of one mine from a takeover offer for 'security' reasons, Oz Minerals sold all but one of its operating mines to the Chinese state-owned minerals trading company Minmetals.

The world's third largest mining company, the Anglo-Australian Rio Tinto, entered an agreement under which the Chinese aluminium producer Chinalco would inject $19 billion and take a substantial equity position. This was later abandoned as commodity markets strengthened towards the middle of 2009.

The discussions of the flow of Chinese equity capital into Rio Tinto and Oz Minerals were two of many in Australia, and in many other resource exporting countries. China was using its strong financial position, with foreign exchange reserves far in excess of any economic policy need for them, to buy into sound assets on favourable terms. For the companies absorbing the capital, this was a financial lifeline—a chance to maintain investment and production and in some cases solvency when the freezing or increased cost of bank finance made business as usual impossible. For the home governments of the companies receiving the equity investment, it was an alternative to the old, broken channels for moving capital from countries where savings exceeded requirements, to those in deficit. For the deficit countries with exportable natural resources, it was a partial alternative to the radical retrenchment of expenditure, employment and living standards that would otherwise have been forced by the drying up of capital flows through the banks.

Whatever its merits, the sudden large increase in proposals for Chinese direct investment generated political controversy in Australia. However, the capital inflows were generally welcomed in developing countries.

A Downward Spiral of Production and Trade

Recessionary impulses spread quickly around the world with the decline in trade. As economic output fell in the countries hit by recession, their imports fell, and so did the exports of their trading partners. As production, incomes and expenditure fell in the trading partners, their own imports fell, feeding into reductions of exports everywhere. And so the world descended into a cycle of contracting imports and production.

The decline in global production from the September quarter of 2008 until mid 2009 was larger than the world had ever known over a comparably short period. Over this time, both industrial and total output for the world as a whole fell more rapidly than in the corresponding early stage of the Great Depression.[8]

The contraction in trade was initially most severe in East Asia. In the first six months of the Asian Financial Crisis of the late 1990s, the contraction there was proportionately greater than for the world in the Great Depression. For East Asia, the decline in the first six months after the Great Crash of 2008 was greater than in the corresponding period of the Asian Financial Crisis.

The League of Nations illustrated the decline in world trade after the Great Crash of 1929 in a 'cobweb spiral' diagram made famous by its reproduction in Kindleberger's history of the Great Depression.[9] Starting from a high point in world trade in April 1929, the value of trade imploded. It fell for forty-seven consecutive months until March 1933.

Figure 7.3 superimposes the data for the first nine months following the world trade peak in June 2008 on Kindleberger's cobweb spiral for the Great Depression. As in 1929, the level of trade spirals in upon itself in 2008 and early 2009. But the spiral is much tighter through the

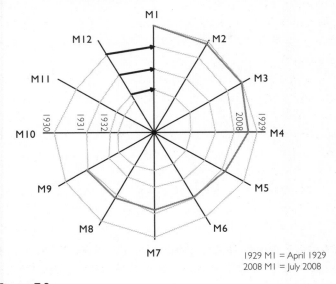

Contracting Spiral of Trade
Comparison of 2008–2009 World Trade and 1929–1933 World Trade

1929 M1 = April 1929
2008 M1 = July 2008

Figure 7.3

Sources: League of Nations, *Monthly Bulletin of Statistics*, February 1934, p. 51
(From Charles P. Kindleberger, *The World in Depression 1929–1939*, Allen Lane
London, 1973, p.173 & OECD Statistics database.

Great Crash of 2008 than in the Great Depression. By
March 2009, world trade had fallen proportionately by
as much as in the first twenty-one months of contraction
in 1929, 1930 and 1931.

By the end of 2008, governments and people everywhere were aware that they were living through a global
recessionary episode of unprecedented dimensions.

8

Bailout

IN LATE 2008, THE governor of the Reserve Bank of Australia (RBA), Glenn Stevens, said in a speech to Australian economists:

> I don't know anyone who predicted this course of events. This should give us cause to reflect on how hard a job it is to make genuinely useful forecasts. What we have seen is truly a 'tail' outcome—the kind of outcome that the routine forecasting process never predicts.[1]

Self-reflection is welcome and necessary in public officials. Good government is evolutionary. However, Stevens' statement misses the point. While admitting a failure to foresee the crisis, he also delineates it as a one-off, an eccentricity of history.

History tells a different story. Time and again, booms have emerged and given way to bust, panic and recession, or worse, in the real economy. They sometimes begin with easy credit—a product of domestic monetary policy, or easier availability of foreign money, or financial innovation. They may have their origins in exaggerated enthusiasm about the commercial benefits of some innovation. Or they may emerge from the tendency of humans towards excessive optimism when things are going well, and excessive pessimism when things turn. They may be encouraged by society's elevation of the gambler to seer when things have gone well for a while.

There were many signs that any one of several distortions and imbalances in the early twenty-first century could generate a difficult adjustment in the Anglosphere. There were credible warnings of the possibility of catastrophic change.[2] No-one predicted exactly the process through which things fell apart. But that is an old story, the story of one thing going wrong and triggering another, with cascading effects on the financial system and the economy.

It is now history that the warnings were ignored. As the boom in housing and financial markets and the global imbalances became larger and larger, policymakers and market participants ignored the manifold risks for which the historical record provided warnings. They preferred boom-time wisdom: this time, things are different. Modern meta-finance had removed the old risks. Given the many large risks, this sanguine view of officials and market participants can be seen as the 'tail' event.

Even as the crisis began, the belief persisted that this time it would not be severe. US Treasury Secretary Hank Paulson and Federal Reserve Governor Ben Bernanke persistently underestimated the extent of the crisis. British Prime Minister Gordon Brown had obviously not foreseen events when he ran the British Treasury into high deficits in the boom preceding the Crash.

East Asian governments had difficulty recognising that their own policies had contributed to the problems. Chinese Premier Wen Jiabao told a morality tale of Western profligacy. South-East Asian and Korean governments oscillated between amazement and schadenfreude over the fact that the United States was in a position similar to their own during the Asian Financial Crisis.

It was not just accountability that was lost in this failure to admit failure. Because officials did not join the dots that connected the Crash, their responses were often more tactical than strategic. One consequence is that many of the systemic problems that created the Great Crash remain in place as this book goes to press.

The global financial policy response played out in three phases. The first sought to arrest the collapse of the shadow banking system and reverse its spread into traditional banking. It began by easing monetary policy and quickly escalated into the leveraging of public balance sheets for a dizzying array of bailouts. The second phase, which focused on the real economy, required a return to Depression Economics. There was general application of Keynesian stimulus to moderate the collapse in global demand, which is the subject of Chapter 9. The third phase was defined by an eclectic list of changes that was long enough to include the de facto return of protectionist policy, changes at the International Monetary Fund (IMF), and diffuse attempts to create new global banking rules.

Too Big to Fail, Too Big to Save

In 1998, the uber-hedge fund Long Term Capital Management (LTCM) melted down. Outsized bets in derivative markets surrounding Russian debt went sour after contagion from the Asian Financial Crisis. LTCM's bets, which were supposed to 'hedge' or offset each other, were so large that they threatened to spark a chain reaction of defaults across global banking. To avert the disaster, then Federal Reserve Chairman Alan Greenspan summoned Wall Street CEOs to his office and organised a bailout for the firm. To ensure this worked, the Federal Reserve lowered short-term interest rates. The too-big-to-fail policy, born in earlier failures of conventional banks, was extended generally to financial institutions.[3]

Too-big-to-fail is the notion that key international financial institutions, especially those that inhabit Wall Street, are so large and enmeshed through derivatives that a regular bankruptcy process would cause cascading failures across the world. It is a measure of the spell cast upon American regulators by the idea that markets are self-correcting, that the LTCM episode did not prompt an urgent reappraisal of their role. LTCM showed clearly that shadow banking had grown to the extent that the failure of one institution could threaten the system. Yet no effort was made to extend or re-create the regulatory umbrella. Nothing was done to provide clear, legally defined support for those that were too-big-to-fail, with regulation to ensure that the public risk was both small and clearly understood. Nor was there an effort to reduce the size of the financial conglomerates or address their interconnections.

By saving LTCM, US authorities made it clear to shadow banking players of all stripes that if their shaky edifice of leverage were ever threatened, then the 'Greenspan put' would be available to them. The LTCM bailout created circumstances in which the shadow banking system's intrinsic recklessness was encouraged by an implied government guarantee. The fact that the bailout solved the immediate problem, apparently at a low cost, entrenched the new approach.

A decade later, this implied guarantee was called on by all and sundry. As the unravelling of shadow banking gathered pace through 2007, Bernanke's Federal Reserve introduced successive monetary innovations that expanded the role it played for traditional banks: as the lender of last resort. At first, the interventions genuflected to the old distinction between deposit-taking institutions (which were expected to receive support) and high-leverage shadow banks (for which there was no obligation to provide support). For example, in December 2007, the Federal Reserve offered loans to deposit-taking banks to provide continued funding for illiquid or impaired securities. This was made available only to those banks that had deposits including those that had also engaged in shadow banking methods. The facility loaned cash against impaired securities, and the interest rate on the loan was determined by auction.

However, in March 2008, the Federal Reserve made new loans to the nineteen banks that acted as dealers for the sale of US Treasury bonds around the world. Five of these were the US investment banks at the heart of shadow banking. The Federal Reserve was now also providing liquidity support to pure shadow banks. The line that had been drawn between monetary support for deposit-taking banks and shadow banks had been crossed.

By mid March, it was clear that Bernanke's innovative efforts to restore the shadow banking system were failing. The housing crash and closure of securitisation markets could not be reversed, and the run on Bear Stearns demanded more direct action. So Treasury Secretary Hank Paulson and his deputy Neel Kashkari oversaw the sale of Bear Stearns to a competitor, JPMorgan, behind closed doors across a weekend. The deal was sealed by a $29 billion loan from the Federal Reserve that was secured against $30 billion of Bear Stearns' non-performing securities. These were floated into a separate company called Maiden Lane. JPMorgan was kept on the hook only for the first $1 billion of losses, which was just as well for the august firm—by April 2009, the securities held within Maiden Lane had been written down by around 38 per cent, with the losses absorbed by the Federal Reserve.

Bear Stearns held derivative positions totalling $13.4 trillion, many of which offset each other. Using the Bank of International Settlements rule of thumb of 2 per cent of the notional level, Bear Stearns had about $270 billion of net exposure. Losses of this magnitude in an environment of panic would have been the trigger for a succession of failures in financial institutions. So Bernanke and Paulson can be seen as having had little choice in the state-subsidised sale of Bear Stearns. It is common practice around the world for authorities to seize a failing bank and sell it quickly to a competitor. It makes sense to short-circuit any potential bank run or the spread of uncertainty to other banks.

But there was a cost. Bear Stearns was a highly lever-aged investment bank and a central pillar of the shadow banking system. The subsidised buyout increased the moral hazard embodied in the too-big-to-fail regime in two ways. First, the organised purchase by JPMorgan, supported by loans and guarantees channelled through Maiden Lane, saved bond holders from any loss. Equity holders took major losses but were not wiped out. A standard insolvency would have involved some combi-nation of discounting investor debt and a debt-for-equity swap defined in a bankruptcy court. The episode did not encourage the future caution of creditors.

Second, the merger with JPMorgan created an even larger institution that combined deposit-taking with investment banking. This completed the extinction of the old division between the two. In the words of Assistant Treasury Secretary Phillip Swagel:

> Moral hazard was a huge concern, but the feeling at Treasury was that even when the Bear transaction was renegotiated up from $2 per share to $10, the loss of wealth was still large enough to give pause to market participants and thus mitigate the moral hazard. Of course, there was moral hazard more

broadly from the fact that Bear's bondholders and
counterparties did not suffer a loss. But Treasury
and the Fed saw little alternative to rescuing the
firm at that time (or least cushioning its fall),
simply because the speed of its collapse left markets
unprepared.[4]

Swagel's description clearly highlights the problem
that faced regulators after twenty years of ignoring the
convergence of shadow and regular banks. Regulators
were no longer making judgements on a clear set of
guidelines for bank solvency. It had become a game of
guessing general market sentiment in the face of the
unravelling of a giant firm.

The Bear Stearns rescue was successful in so far as it
calmed markets for six months. However, the warning
presented by the collapse was ignored. No new insolvency
process emerged for dealing with systemically important
shadow banks. Come September 2008, this failure and the
arbitrariness of regulation became a shattering problem.
As the run on shadow banks intensified following the
nationalisation of the government-sponsored enterprises,
it became clear that all of the investment banks at the
heart of securitisation were doomed. Another too-big-
to-fail deal was struck over a weekend when Merrill
Lynch was shepherded into the fold of Bank of America.
At the time, the merger was considered market-based.
Scandal erupted later amid accusations of coercion by
government.

Over the same weekend during which the Merrill
Lynch deal took place, executives of Lehman Brothers

also negotiated with several possible buyers, notably Barclays. In this case, the Treasury and Federal Reserve elected not to support the deal with guarantees. To make the difference, the guarantees would have had to be immense, even by the extraordinary standards set so recently with Bear Stearns. Without them, Barclays walked away and Lehman Brothers went bust. Again, we can refer to Treasury insider Phillip Swagel: 'The feeling at Treasury was that Lehman's management had been given abundant warning that no federal assistance was in the offing, and market participants were aware of this and had time to prepare'.

Swagel's testimony is revealing. Whether markets had sufficient time to prepare for a Lehman bankruptcy should be beside the point. Like it or not, too-big-to-fail was now the functional regime. The judgement of both Paulson and Bernanke that Lehman Brothers should be let go to avoid moral hazard harked back to a long-redundant system that separated deposit-taking banks and shadow banks. This was a regime that authorities had systematically undermined by enabling traditional banks to become involved in shadow banking activities, and by playing active roles in the rescue of LTCM and Bear Stearns. It is no wonder that the markets were shocked. A financial system will be shocked from time to time if it is not based on transparent rules that are enforced.

Before the month was out, American Insurance Group (AIG) and Citigroup were both saved using a similar combination of gigantic Federal Reserve loans, off-balance-sheet vehicles, fiscal guarantees and insurance wraps. Again, regulators probably had little choice. The companies at risk were so vast and interconnected, and the markets so gripped by panic, that their failures would have caused a meltdown of global proportions.

Any pretence of a division between shadow and deposit-taking banks was dropped when the remaining investment banks, Morgan Stanley and Goldman Sachs, were permitted to transform themselves into bank holding companies. This designation had formerly been reserved for deposit-taking institutions. The melange was baked by December, when the pure shadow bank financing arm of General Motors, GMAC, was permitted to become a bank holding company.

The Federal Reserve now extended its lending facilities in the form of non-recourse loans to the money-market funds, so that they could resume purchases of short-term corporate debt. It also purchased short-term corporate debt directly through a Special Purpose Vehicle. The Federal Reserve was now the lender and buyer of last resort for the shadow banking conveyor belt, while the Federal Deposit Insurance Corporation (FDIC) guaranteed the senior debt of all deposit-taking institutions and their holding companies.

The various arms of the US Government now stretched around the country's entire shadow and traditional financial system. Through incremental decisions the regulatory umbrella now covered everyone.

The Bailout Goes Nuclear

Equity and credit markets didn't respond. Investors had concluded that the entire US banking system might be insolvent. The Dow Jones Index continued to sink to new lows. So Hank Paulson played his final card. Faced with an equity market calamity, he determined that a systemic solution to the crisis was needed. Paulson lobbied the US Congress to provide $700 billion to purchase toxic assets that were clogging the arteries of finance. Again, he opted for opacity and discretion over transparency and law.

Paulson's initial proposal was rejected on these grounds. Democrats and Republicans alike sallied against the use of public finances to bail out private banking operations, and the lack of accountability written into the proposal. Republican Jeb Hensarling, following his self-described 'principles of faith, family, free enterprise, and freedom', rejected the proposal on the grounds it was 'the slippery slope to socialism'. The pastoral Texan waxed that it would leave the nation with 'the mother of all debt'.[5] Another dissenting Texas Republican, the square-jawed, plump and bespectacled John Culberson, dubbed Paulson 'King Henry', pilfering a *Newsweek* cover line from the previous week.

Many congressmen mentioned that it was the furious abuse of everyday taxpayers pouring into their offices that gave them pause. Ordinary Americans were being offered no help as the banks foreclosed on their homes, and they made their unhappiness known to the congressmen who were contemplating enormous subsidies to the banks that were taking away these homes.[6] However, after Congress rejected Paulson's plan, the Dow Jones Index fell 778 points, its largest ever one-day points fall. The plan was renovated and passed within four days.

Fierce criticism of the initiative continued. Economists Paul Krugman and Nouriel Roubini asked why, if the United States was supplying fiscal support to banks, should they not be nationalised? Both argued for a 'Swedish solution', making reference to Sweden's successful nationalisations and eventual reprivatisations following their own financial crisis in the early 1990s. Those institutions that passed a sustainability test could be supported with additional capital, with government receiving equity for the funds provided; those that failed could be put through government-supported bankruptcies. Krugman and Roubini wanted to create a too-big-to-fail insolvency regime that mitigated moral hazard through clear rules. It would protect the public interest in a functioning financial system without protecting the investors who had made the mistakes that had created the risks.

Instead, Paulson's plan made matters even more murky. It was described by one Republican as a 'mud sandwich'. Within weeks it diverged from its intended purpose. Through rapid mutation, it became a generalised capital replenishment program for the top fifteen banks, virtually all of which were, to varying degrees, responsible for the crisis. By the end of November 2008, 106 traditional and shadow banks had received support.[7]

Over subsequent months, the mutation continued. The $700 billion was used to support GMAC, as well as to provide support for the failing carmakers themselves: Chrysler and General Motors. Too-big-to-fail now applied to industrial enterprises. Few company managers were fired and, despite the urgings of the public, no board members lost seats. Sporadic attempts were made to limit executive remuneration for recipients of the largesse, but these were ineffectual.

A new Democrat President, Barack Obama, was elected in November 2008 and sworn into office in January 2009. He inherited $10.5 trillion of US government bailouts, guarantees and liquidity facilities; there was evidence of stabilisation in equity markets and signs of slow life in the debt markets. The interventions had deeply entrenched the too-big-to-fail paradigm and its associated moral hazards. The top twenty banks had been reduced to fifteen. The government remained the sole sponsor of securitisation markets. Those responsible for the crisis were enmeshed more intimately than ever with the officials whose job it was to set the rules by which they were to operate.

A New Hope

If the too-big-to-fail bailout of the US financial system was not yet irreversible as the new Obama administration took power in early 2009, it did not take long to become so. New appointees to key positions carried on the Greenspan–Rubin era.

In January, Larry Summers, long-time deputy to Robert Rubin and his successor as Treasury secretary for Clinton, moved in as the main economic adviser in the White House.

The dour, intellectually rigorous nephew of two Nobel prize-winning economists, and a gruff non-diplomat, Summers had gone back to Harvard to become the university's president when Bush moved to Washington. He was drummed out by feminist reaction to outrageous statements on female intellect, and so found time to do well in a New York hedge fund on his way back to the capital.

The new Treasury secretary was Tim Geithner, a Summers understudy during the Clinton presidency.

Both Summers and Geithner had had experience with previous financial meltdowns. Most particularly they had played key roles in the global policy response to the Asian Financial Crisis.

Dr Chalongphob Sussangkarn was Thailand's finance minister in the aftermath of the crisis. In May 2009, he recalled how Summers and Geithner had identified the interaction of corruption and nepotism with flaws in financial regulation as the crux of the emergency. This diagnosis dominated the perspectives of the IMF, the World Bank and bilateral donors, which all prescribed retrenchment in public expenditure to restore budgetary balance, and the quick closure of insolvent financial institutions.

Chalongphob commented that Summers had been right on the diagnosis but wrong on the prescription. He also noted that the same diagnosis that had been applied to the Asian Financial Crisis was relevant now to the United States, observing that it seemed that Summers and Geithner had learned from their mistakes and were offering the opposite prescription in their home country.

This point of view was reinforced in the same month by Indonesian Finance Minister Sri Mulyani. She noted that 'KKN'—corruption, cronyism and nepotism—were responsible for the Indonesian crisis and went on: 'I have told Tim [Geithner] that he only has to read the same rule book that he read to us a decade ago. On what was wrong, of course, and not on what to do about it'.[8]

Treasury Secretary Geithner seemed to be moving towards these perspectives in a statement in June 2009. He introduced Treasury controls on remuneration in financial institutions that were dependent upon government support. According to the *New York Times*, Geithner said that 'the financial crisis had many significant causes, but executive compensation practices were a contributing factor. Incentives for short-term gains overwhelmed the checks and balances meant to mitigate against the risk of excess leverage'.[9]

Summers also acknowledged the force of the South-East Asian perspectives. In an interview with the *Financial Times* that touched on US Treasury prescriptions during the Asian Financial Crisis he admitted:

> There have been moments, certainly, when I under-stood better some of the reactions of officials in crisis countries now than one was able to from the outside at the time. It is easier to be for more radical solutions when one lives thousands of miles away than when it is one's own country.[10]

Whatever the heartburn, Summers and Geithner pursued the familiar policy of leveraging the government's balance sheet to restore shadow banking. In some ways, the plans were even less transparent than before. Geithner first used much of the remaining Paulson funds to create the Public Private Investment Partnership (PPIP). This program used a government subsidy of almost 80 per cent to lure private capital into buying the toxic assets that were the source of the banks' apparent insolvency. The scheme was praised in some quarters for its innovation—Nouriel Roubini, a staunch critic of the Paulson approach, praised the attempt to engage private capital in the rescue. But Paul Krugman criticised it as just another bailout, with elaborate engineering thrown in to disguise its real nature. It was also criticised as an opportunity for banks to manipulate outcomes at the expense of the taxpayer. Then, in March, a decision was made to ease mark-to-market (or fair value) accounting rules. This was endorsed for global application at a Group of 20 meeting in early April.

The Columbia University economist Joseph Stiglitz pointed out that the juxtaposition of the two initiatives continued the opaque and confused thinking of regulators. The PPIP was designed to free bank balance sheets of toxic assets, yet the changes to accounting rules encouraged banks to hold onto them. This contradiction became manifest by June as the PPIP had little uptake in the markets.

Like many of the emerging policy responses to the Great Crash, there was a case for the suspension of mark-to-market rules, but there was also a high cost. In a chaotic market, today's market value of an asset will sometimes be a small fraction of what it will become when markets settle. Firms that are required to mark-to-market the value of their assets may be revealed as insolvent when they would be solvent at 'normal' valuations. Insolvency has many costs for others and disrupts real economic activity. There is a rationale for avoiding it when it is unnecessary.

However, in the absence of mark-to-market rules, there is no objective way to value assets. Discretion must play a role. A firm can hide the low value of some assets and hold onto them in the hope that something will turn up to increase their value—you never know your luck in a big city. Companies that are truly insolvent on any reasonable and informed assessment can hide the reality.

It is commonly and reasonably said that the long economic stagnation of Japan through the 1990s resulted from a failure to recognise losses in asset value early and clearly. This left the banks holding overvalued assets and acting with extreme caution while they waited for something to turn up. The problems of the Japanese banks can be contrasted with those of the Anglosphere banks that also suffered deep losses in the value of their assets during the 1990–91 recession. Taking the losses immediately to profit accounts and balance sheets was initially disruptive. It exacerbated short-term costs, but led to a much stronger and more durable recovery. In the more severe circumstances of the Great Crash of 2008, the United States opted for the grinding Japanese approach.

In early 2009 the Federal Reserve was moving further into uncharted waters. On 18 March, following a lead from the Bank of England, it approved purchases of $1.7 trillion of various securities, including Fannie Mae and Freddie Mac debt and mortgage-backed securities, plus $300 billion of US Treasury bonds; that is, it began printing money to underpin domestic economic activity. One effect was to raise doubts about the long-term value of US financial assets among East Asian investors.

The surviving banks could now earn historically high margins for traditional banking business. Their cost of funds was now low owing to the low official rates, the government guarantee on new debt, and the way in which the caution of the times flooded traditional banks with new deposits. Dramatically reduced competition in mortgage origination and a new refinancing boom delivered solid new business to the banks. The cherry on the cake came from the rescue and virtual nationalisation of AIG, which in winding down its derivatives book was paying out huge sums to the counterparty banks to close out contracts. The banks reported much higher than expected earnings for the first quarter of 2009 and their share prices enjoyed a sparkling rally—the Standard & Poor's Financial Index doubled from a low of 82 in March to 164 in June. These earnings were manufactured by the US Government.

Questions still abounded about the banks' prospects for genuine commercial profits. Some anxiety was eased by a formal series of stress tests conducted by 150 regulatory officials on nineteen banks over March and April, which indicated that the banks needed to raise an additional $75 billion to bolster their capital reserves. Analysts and close observers were critical of the ways in which the tests were negotiated and applied, and of the variations across firms, but nevertheless they helped to increase banking confidence. Several banks immediately issued new shares to cover shortfalls identified by the test, and several were also able to issue new bonds.

The stabilisation gave the Obama administration a window in which to begin rethinking the future of the regulatory environment. The challenge facing the new government and its Treasury secretary was to deal with a Great Crash elephant that had been corralled and sedated but in no way diminished.

Wall Street took no chances—the *New York Times* began reporting unprecedentedly high donations from the financial sector to Congressional Democrats, as the new administration and Congress grappled with the need for tighter regulation of banking.[11]

As this book was going to press, the US Treasury proposed a broad overhaul of its regulatory structures. The proposal contained five major measures. To begin with, derivatives were to be brought onto transparent trading exchanges. The recommendation excluded bespoke contracts—these tailor-made agreements made up the bulk of the credit default swap (CDS) market that had been at the heart of the shadow bank meltdown. These would require reporting and higher capital reserves. Professor of Law at the University of San Diego, Frank Partnoy, described this as a 'dangerous loophole'.[12]

Next, the large banks that traded CDSs and other interconnecting derivatives—contributing greatly to their too-big-to-fail status—were to be subject to new regulatory powers governed by the Federal Reserve. Given the Federal Reserve's role in precipitating the crisis, Congress and many commentators expressed deep reservation about an increase in its powers. Moreover, much of the new supervision would be managed behind closed doors, sealing already intimate regulators and regulatees in a cocoon that did nothing to address capture.

A new insolvency regime for systemically important or too-big-to-fail banks was also suggested. It would operate along similar lines to the FDIC and its insolvency processes for regular banks. The proposal implicitly acknowledged defeat of the idea that too-big-to-fail banks should be broken up. Additionally, the role of rating agencies in assessing the credit risk of securities was to be watered down; no comprehensive reform of the agencies' conflicts of interest was proposed.

Finally, securities issuers were to be forced to retain a portion of their issued tranches to increase their responsibility for the pass-through product. Given that the crisis was triggered by the retention of these very securities, the measure left much to be desired.

Little mention was made of executive remuneration.

Australian Bailout

In the early days of October 2008, money poured into the big four Australian banks from other financial institutions. But life was becoming increasingly anxious for them as well. One by one they advised the government that they were having difficulty rolling over their foreign debts. Several sought and received meetings with Prime Minister Rudd. The banks told him that, if the government did not guarantee their foreign debts, they would not be able to roll over the debt as it became due. Some was due immediately, so they would have to begin withdrawing credit from Australian borrowers. They would be insolvent sooner rather than later.

To be sure, a sudden and extreme freeze on credit, perhaps enforced by the insolvency of the banks, would end the Australian current account deficit. Spending would fall sharply, and with it the value of imports. The awful reliability of the market process in removing an external deficit once financing dried up was demonstrated in Australia when domestic booms funded by foreign debt ended abruptly with depression in the early 1890s and 1930s. It was demonstrated just as clearly in the Asian Financial Crisis. But the process of adjustment would be enormously disruptive and costly.

The government quickly formed the view that the avoidance of a sudden adjustment through the automatic market process was a worthy object of policy. On 12 October it announced that, for a small fee, it would guarantee the banks' new wholesale liabilities. This would include the huge rollovers of old foreign debt as it matured. The government also announced a guarantee on all deposits up to A$1 million. All four banks expressed their thanks and relief in a joint meeting with the Prime Minister on 23 October. This became law in November.

There was relatively little public comment on the guarantee of wholesale funding, with *The Australian*'s experienced economic columnist Henry Thornton being a rare exception. Much more attention was given to the less significant partial guarantee of bank deposits.

Australia was engulfed by a different kind of crisis than that consuming other Anglosphere countries. In the United States, falling asset prices had triggered the collapse of shadow banking. In the United Kingdom, the fallout from that collapse had undermined the larger banks whose assets had been devalued, or which had depended on the continued reliability of the shadow banking mechanisms. The subsequent withdrawal of credit undermined the United Kingdom's own housing market. In Australia, however, the difficulties were on the liability side of bank balance sheets. Banks had become heavily reliant on foreign borrowing and suddenly they were unable to borrow abroad. The non-banks had had no buyers for their securities for almost a year.

There are no degrees of insolvency. A firm is just as insolvent if it is not able to meet its financial obligations as they fall due because it cannot roll over debt, as it is if the value of the assets in its balance sheet is deeply impaired. The difference is that the problem on the liability side is much more easily (and in most cases cheaply) repaired by a guarantee than the problem on the asset side. The sudden risk of insolvency in Australian banking was simply a more tractable problem than those experienced by other Anglosphere nations.

The banks might counter that they only needed the guarantee because other governments around the world were guaranteeing the debts of their national banks. This does not sit easily against the survival of banks without wholesale funding guarantees in many countries where banks had stayed within the old operational templates— for example Australia's neighbours Indonesia and Papua New Guinea. In any case, this avoids the point. The Australian banks' dependence on government-guaranteed debt was exceptional: in July 2009, Australian banks accounted for 10 per cent of the world's government-guaranteed debt.[13] Through foreign borrowing to support domestic lending, the big four Australian banks were active, enthusiastic participants in the global shadow banking system that was now unravelling.

The double guarantee stabilised the major banks. And before long they had several more reasons to smile. The new deposit guarantee immediately exacerbated a run on the mortgage trust sector that competed with them for conservative depositor funds. The run forced many of the funds to freeze redemptions.

The fate of the mortgage trusts was controversial, but it obscured the much more far-reaching problems arising from the guarantee covering the banks' wholesale funding needs. The guarantee was structured much like the US monoline insurers. The government loaned its AAA rating to the banks for a fee. This 'insurance wrap' made the same compromises of private sector banking rules that had afflicted the US bailouts. As Henry Thornton made clear: 'If a wealthy entrepreneur had provided the bailout (as Kerry Packer did for Westpac in the previous crisis) he would have taken a large slice of equity in return. Why should Australia's taxpayers not get equity for the bank bailout in this crisis?'[14]

At first, the subsidiaries and branches of foreign banks were excluded, as were second-tier banks, and they lost deposits to the big four. Then they complained at the different treatment and were subsequently included. By March 2009 it was clear that the guarantee had made it difficult for state governments to attract investors to their debt. In short order, the federal government guaranteed state government borrowing as well, adding to its growing off-balance sheet commitments.

The Rudd government also extended its fiscal support to a program of buyer-of-last-resort for the rest of the shadow banking sector. This support had begun prior to the bank debt guarantee with a commitment to buy $4 billion dollars worth of Australian residential mortgage-backed securities through the Australian Office of Financial Management, a figure that was eventually doubled. The initiative had some success in clearing the bank warehouses of non-bank loans waiting to be securitised and threw security issues a lifeline.

As the Australian Government turned to fiscal expansion to fight the downturn in real economic activity, part of the stimulus was focused on the asset side of the banks' balance sheets—the loans secured against housing and commercial real estate. In October 2008, the government announced a A$10.4 billion stimulus package. It included a doubling of the First Home Owners Grant to A$14 000, with an additional A$7000 grant if it related to a new house. In January 2009, the Rudd government's asset bailout was extended to commercial real estate in the Australian Business Investment Partnership (ABIP). It began life with $2 billion from the federal Budget, as well as $500 million each from the big four banks. A former NAB executive was appointed to head ABIP and he was authorised to borrow up to $26 billion, guaranteed again by the government's AAA rating, to be used for loans to what he described as viable commercial projects. The initiative bore the hallmarks of regulatory compromise that were familiar from the United States—it was not active at the time this book went to print.

The collapse of US financial institutions also left a vacuum in the provision of motor vehicle retail financing in Australia, at a time when demand for vehicles was falling precipitously. The government announced a $2 billion Australian dollar facility (OzCar) to support the extension of credit to motor vehicle purchasers. As with ABIP, by mid 2009 the facility had not yet been activated.

Just as in the United States, the various Australian interventions stabilised the major banks. The mergers of small banks with large ones, the departure of American and European banks, and the collapse of non-bank competition drastically reduced competition in all Australian financial services. The competitive achievements of a quarter-century of deregulation were reversed and much more in six months. The big four banks now controlled more than 74 per cent of the total mortgage market, and rising swiftly.[15] This compared with a low point below 60 per cent before the crisis.

The big four used their much greater market power. They increased fees across business and consumer lending, as well as gross margins on loans. In June, the RBA reported that margins for mortgage lending had risen in the period of financial turbulence.[16] In an early glimpse of a brave new world of oligopolistic financing, analysts were expecting much higher profits from banking operations in the first half of 2009.[17]

The great mercy for Australians is that their banks' potentially fatal problems could be managed with much smaller public outlays than those required by US and European financial institutions. The various Australian policy measures, however, did nothing to reduce the reliance on foreign wholesale borrowing that had quietly invited the Great Crash elephant into Australia. From November 2008 to May 2009, the four major banks took onto their balance sheets $104.1 billion of government-guaranteed external debt.[18]

Bulletproof

Why is it that, with Australia an exuberant member of the Anglosphere in many respects, the value of its banking assets held up much better than in other bubble-afflicted economies? This is an important question, and not only for Australians. There may be valuable lessons in the Australian experience for the regulation of modern finance everywhere.

First, we must acknowledge that the falls were still large in Australia and that they are not all over. Many non-bank financial institutions in Australia fared as badly as their North American counterparts. In June 2009, veteran bank analyst Brian Johnson estimated that the big four banks would sustain more than A$13 billion in loan losses in the 2009 financial year. Virtually no loan losses are expected for residential real estate lending until 2010. This in itself is remarkable given the demolition of housing asset values within US and UK banks.

As we have seen, Australian banks had negligible exposure to bad assets arising from the collapse of shadow banking. They simply did not use securitisation to any degree. Nor had the banks' use of clever money in other parts of their business become regular or

significant, apart from the huge offshore borrowing.
Only NAB had ventured deeply into the purchase and
repackaging of exotic securities. Unlike UK banks, they
therefore avoided fallout in their assets from the near-
collapse of US shadow banking and were not forced
to ration credit. Was this due to prudence, regulation,
different remuneration structures, or perhaps deeper
differences in business culture?

We have already argued that although Australian
banks were slower to adopt the risks of shadow banking,
they were on the same track. By this reckoning, Australia
was saved by the timing of the Great Crash.

An ideological difference may also have been important. Extreme versions of libertarian economic thought
were hardly represented in relevant Australian intellectual life, and not at all in government or the regulatory
agencies. There was no counterpart in official Australia of
Alan Greenspan's views of economic processes. Australian
policy making was generally more autonomous of business money than the American model. Although there
was some movement of senior staff between banks and
regulators, it was mainly from the public into the private sector. The Australian regulatory agencies always
saw a central role for prudential regulation in the financial sector, including at the height of the enthusiasm for
deregulation in the 1980s.

Some commentators have drawn attention to
Australian banks' conservative culture as a factor in
mitigating their loan losses. This may point to the fact
that Australian business and political culture in general
was less taken with the extremes of individual wealth
accumulation than the United States. This difference was

evident in the countries' contrasting approaches to the emergence of risky and fraudulent practices in mortgage lending in the early twenty-first century.

A frenzy did grow around 'get rich' schemes based on highly leveraged investment in housing. The promoters of the schemes fuelled the mania with false information, 'how to' packages for naive investors, and proposals on access to finance. The schemes had much in common with the raw edge of funding for mortgage lending in the United States and the United Kingdom at that time. The RBA responded by warning investors of the risks in the housing market. *The Sydney Morning Herald* and *The Age* newspapers in 2003 went to considerable lengths to expose fraudulent representations to investors, and regulatory agencies followed up on the media reports.[19] The corresponding action by the US Federal Reserve was to laud the expansion of subprime lending for housing, while the national media and regulatory agencies were generally inactive.

In discussing the differences in business and political culture between Australia and other parts of the Anglosphere, RBA Governor Glenn Stevens has drawn attention to Australia's searing experiences with two earlier financial sector failures.[20]

The years immediately after the deregulation of Australian banking in the 1980s saw a sharp reduction in lending standards, as foreign and domestic banks battled for market share and income. This contributed to a boom in asset prices, which was brought to heel by tight monetary policies at the end of the decade. This, in turn, precipitated deep recession, during which Australian banks incurred loan losses equivalent to 5 per cent of

GDP; these losses were proportionately larger than those experienced by US or UK banks during their recessions of the early 1990s. Two of the four major Australian banks suffered near-death experiences; two of the five banks owned by state governments were absorbed by other entities, with the governments covering huge losses. The Australian regulators were left with high sensitivity to banking risk.

Australia also had its version of a major failure in the insurance industry long before America's AIG. The failure of HIH in 2001 had all of the elements of the Great Crash in the United States: weak regulatory arrangements; incentive structures that encouraged senior executives to risk their businesses for personal gain; advisers who were compromised by conflicts of interest; even a prominent part for Goldman Sachs through its Australian subsidiary. HIH was then, and still is, the largest corporate failure in Australian history. It led directly to the strengthening of a single financial sector regulator which helped to keep the systemic risks associated with partial regulation out of Australia.

A third experience should be added. The Asian Financial Crisis greatly damaged Australia's main trading partners in East Asia. Australia worked closely with governments in South-East Asian countries and South Korea over their response to the crisis. Australia's currency and other financial markets were subject to speculative attacks by North Atlantic hedge funds in much the same way as were the financial markets of East Asia.

The Australian and East Asian policymakers and regulators shared doubts about the simple-minded prescriptions of the US Treasury and the institutions under its influence. Australian officials emerged from the episode with clearer views on the importance of regulation to constrain destabilising speculation and financial sector risk. The US agencies learned no such lessons until their own experience in the Great Crash.

But let us remember that all was not well in the Australian financial system. Australian banks engaged in their own dramatic expansion of shadow banking activities in the form of a vast increase in offshore borrowing, which fuelled an explosion of lending for housing and consumption. This contributed to an increase in housing prices similar to the average of the Anglosphere. As the global crisis intensified through late 2007 and 2008, these prices threatened to unwind, falling 4.5 per cent nationally,[21] a figure almost double the fall experienced in the United States market in its first year of declining prices.[22] This all would have been fatal during the Crash if it had not been for timely intervention by the Australian Government. The support was on a scale and of a kind that would have stunned any informed observer in advance of the Great Crash.

Ultimately, two policy initiatives played key roles in stemming the fall in asset values. The first, a monetary initiative, was when the RBA cut its interest rate to 3 per cent. Other Anglosphere nations had also cut rates to very low levels but these had been close to the same low rates during the brief recession of 2001. In Australia the low rates had not been seen for nearly half a century. The second, fiscal intervention was the Rudd government's First Home Buyers Grant. Large grants working as house deposits had a big effect in 2009 in halting and then reversing a housing correction.

In the first quarter of 2009, a flood of first-home buyers washed through the housing market. *The Australian* reported that the average loan size for first-home buyers rose A$29 500 to an average of A$280 600 in the six months following the grant. By February 2009, 26.9 per cent of buyers were purchasing their first home, up from 17.3 per cent in February 2008. The number of first-home buyers had also jumped by 50 per cent.

A long period of tepid growth may make the removal of the grant damaging to residential housing. Like so many government interventions in the name of addressing the crisis, it will be difficult to withdraw.

Reprivatisation

As June 2009 rolled around and the stock market rally in bank shares continued, many banks around the world began to agitate for liberation from government support. One motive was the strong public insistence and government acceptance that banks continuing to receive financial support should be subject to controls on remuneration. This concentrated the minds of US banking executives on breaking free of direct budgetary subsidies.

US banks focused upon returning the capital they had received as a part of Paulson's plan, and on 9 June ten banks were granted permission to return the funds. There was little discussion of the other ongoing supports for US banks. The Federal Reserve's innovative loans in return for dubious collateral remained, as did the FDIC's guarantee of all new senior debt issued. Meanwhile, in Australia, several of the major banks had managed to issue some international debt without using the government guarantee, but its ongoing presence influenced market perceptions about the quality of the banks' bonds, and huge and much larger issuance of government-guarateed debt continued.

Governments face continuing large funding burdens in relation to banks. As *The Economist* pointed out, as of early July, Western governments remained in control of $450 billion in bank equity. Over the coming two years, no less than $25.6 trillion of wholesale funding will require refinancing.[23]

The US Government's plan to allow US banks to grow their way out of near or actual insolvency was looking like Japan in the 1990s. Success in the United States depended on the trajectory of the housing market recovery, and on whether new big surprises lay hidden in the immense toxic residue of derivatives sold before the Crash. Success would also depend on the continuation of cheap wholesale funding. This, in turn, was reliant on an ongoing flow of East Asian savings that were being redeployed into domestic demand expansion, and on inflationary expectations. Long bond rates were already rising in June.

There was little prospect of a return to what would once have been seen as normal market dynamics.

9

Depression Economics

FOR A COUPLE OF weeks in August 2008, the people of Beijing marvelled at a blue sky and the occasional clear view of the Western Hills. They told their grandchild that it was just like the old days. Then, after the Olympics closing ceremony, people waited for the factories to begin billowing their smoke again and for the gridlock on the roads to return. People kept waiting, but the skies stayed blue.

Things had changed in the great industrial cities of the coast as well. The warehouses alongside the factories and the wharves were suddenly full. Workers received a message with their fortnightly pay that they weren't needed for a while—the company would tell them when to come back.

The greatest migration in human history went into reverse. Seventy million of the 140 million workers from rural China in China's industrial cities went back to their homes before the usual time at the Spring Festival, which took place in February the following year. Most stayed at home for longer than usual after the feasting.[1] The slump took the Chinese by surprise, just as it surprised the Americans and the Europeans and the Japanese.

Separately and together, the governments of the world set out to relearn the policy lessons of Depression Economics.

Meetings of the Group of 20 (G20) provided one vehicle for this learning. A special Leaders Summit on Financial Markets and the World Economy was convened on 15 November 2008. But it achieved little beyond a commitment to allow no more bankruptcies like Lehman Brothers, and a vague endorsement of fiscal stimulus measures. The Chinese Government used the occasion to highlight a huge fiscal expansion. The meeting's main achievement was itself, a global forum that brought together the surplus and deficit nations.

The reconvening of the G20 in London on 2 April 2009 finished with great fanfare and grandiloquence. British Prime Minister Gordon Brown announced to the world: 'We have resolved that from today we will together manage the process of globalisation ... We have agreed that in doing so we will build a more sustainable and more open and fairer global society'. Beyond the grand rhetoric, at least two major agreements emerged from the meeting. The first was a new set of rules for the International Monetary Fund (IMF), including the validation of the use of fiscal deficits in recessionary circumstances, an increase of the resources available for lending, and greater representation of developing countries in governance. The IMF was strengthened in its capacity to rescue capital-starved developing countries. The second, more far-reaching outcome was the endorsement of global fiscal stimulus measures.

Governments everywhere had turned to the economics of John Maynard Keynes.

Deficient Demand and Unemployment

Dislocation of the global economy caused people to consume less and to save more. It also caused them to invest less.

As the stocks of unsold products rose, and as firms and individuals began to realise the imbalance that was emerging between intended production and intended expenditure, firms reduced production to restore the balance. They stopped investing, because existing capacity was ample to produce all that they could sell. The consequential decline in expenditure exacerbated the surplus of productive capacity over expenditure. At least from September 2008, for the world as a whole, the sum of intentions to save exceeded the sum of intentions to invest by a large margin.

It was the special contribution of Keynes at Cambridge University in the 1930s to demonstrate that the persistent high unemployment of that decade was not a temporary aberration that would be corrected through market processes, but the consequence of a shortfall of domestic demand relative to the productive capacity of the economy that could persist in the absence of corrective action by government.[2] Paul Krugman at Princeton University and *The New York Times* has kept reminding us of the relevance of Keynes, at first to the Japanese recession of the 1990s, and now to the Great Recession.[3]

The classical doctrines of economics had argued that, if markets were left to themselves, real wages and living standards would fall enough in the long run to make investment attractive again, promoting an increase in employment. Maybe, responded Keynes, but the long run might be very long. And in the long run we are all dead.

Keynes's Depression Economics argues for government policy that deliberately increases expenditure towards levels that put to work all the resources of a fully employed economy. It can be increased expenditure by government or by the private sector, on consumption or on investment. The nature of the expenditure may have a big or a small effect on future productivity and living standards, but this is of minor importance to the immediate increase in production, employment and incomes.

Authorities have two principal means of stimulating expenditure. One is to increase the money supply and so reduce short-term interest rates. Long-term interest rates are determined in the market and capture expectations about future inflation, as well as supply and demand for capital. They are not directly reduced through government policy. It is the real interest rate, the rate in the marketplace less the expected rate of inflation, that is most relevant to company decisions on production and investment, and household decisions on consumption.

Reference to the real interest rate, taking inflation into account, introduces a complication. In deep recession, prices can fall, as they did all over the world during the Great Depression. Prices as measured by consumer price indexes are falling in 2009 in many regions, including the United States, Japan, China and the European Union. If prices are falling, a dollar will buy more tomorrow than it will buy today. Once borrowers take into account the likelihood that they will be repaying debt in dollars that are more valuable than they were at the time the loan was taken out, even interest rates that are near zero can be positive in real terms. In any case, once interest rates have fallen to zero, the stimulus that comes from reducing them has reached its limit.

The other way for government to increase total expenditure in the economy is for it to increase its own spending, or to reduce the taxation that it collects from the private sector, which will encourage greater spending in the private sector. Either approach will increase the budget deficit in the first instance. This might be funded by issuing bonds to the public, or by borrowing from the central bank, which is also known as printing money.

While the conditions of Depression Economics persist, the presence of unemployed resources prevents increased expenditure from causing higher inflation. This is true whether the expenditure is induced by lower interest rates, higher government expenditure or lower taxation. It is true whether the government deficit is funded by issuing bonds or by borrowing from the central bank.

The final increase in the budget deficit will not be as high as the initial expectation because in the circumstances of Depression Economics, it will induce higher employment, incomes and expenditure, all of which will contribute to public revenues. Economist Max Corden has demonstrated in a recent paper that for a country with a freely floating exchange rate, and in which monetary policy settings are not changed in response to the larger budget deficit, there should be no expectation that the sum of private and government debt will end up higher after a Depression Economics increase in the budget deficit than it would have been without the stimulus.[4] Independently of the exchange rate regimes, the stimulus should not lead to higher global debt levels (the sum of government and private debt for all countries taken together) than would otherwise have been present.

The Limits of Stimulus

There are limits to these methods of stimulating expenditure. In the longer term, as expenditure increases and unemployment falls, two constraints become important. One is the emergence of inflation, and the other is the cost that raising taxes to service government debt imposes on the economy.

First, once expenditure and employment have begun to expand, they can be mutually reinforcing. As recovery proceeds, sooner or later bottlenecks in supply will begin to appear. Inflationary pressures re-emerge. For the renewed prosperity to be sustainable, the policies that

were established to encourage expenditure have to be
withdrawn, and at some stage put into reverse gear. The
authorities have to slow the growth in expenditure by
raising interest rates and reducing the budget deficit in
some combination.

The second constraint follows from the fact that
large government deficits must eventually pay interest on
debt, and may have to repay the debt itself. However,
the economic cost of servicing debt is not the interest or
loan repayment, but the cost of distorting the decisions
of firms and households, which inevitably accompanies
the raising of taxation.

The first constraint seems obvious enough, but there
is a complication. The expansion of expenditure will
only proceed smoothly until full employment has been
restored, if all of the institutional arrangements in the
economy that determine individual claims on income
and government services add up to the productive
capacity of the economy. But why should this matter if
there was full employment before the Crash? If there
were no change in the institutional arrangements that
determine claims on incomes, and no reduction in the
productive capacity of the economy, why wouldn't the
sum of all of the claims still be within the productive
capacity of the economy? The answer is that the amount
of expenditure that the productive capacity of the global
economy can support is likely to be lower after than
before the Crash.

There are several ways in which this may happen.
The Great Crash was preceded by a bubble in which,
for a while, expenditure and output may have been

unsustainably high (this is more likely to have been an issue in the Anglosphere than in the world generally). In addition, the effervescence of the boom encouraged consumption at the expense of investment.

The collapse of international financial intermediation meant that neither people in the surplus countries nor people in the deficit countries can realise their preferred balance between present and future consumption after the Crash. Those who prefer to spend more now on consumption and investment, and to pay back the deficit later, can not do so. Those who prefer to save more now than they invested, and to spend more later, can not do so either. Those with tendencies to borrow or lend are forced to live more within their current incomes. According to their respective preferences, both are poorer to be so constrained. The Great Crash also reduces the productive capacity of the economy because the collapse of financial systems reduces trade within and especially between countries.

The various dislocations of the Great Crash mean that resources are used less efficiently than when exchange was easier, and the outcomes of investments were more predictable. This reduces the average productivity of economies. As a result, it may not be possible for some time to restore full employment and at the same time to re-establish for all citizens the standards of living that they had before the Crash. If wages, social security payments and all other elements of standards of living are fixed for each individual at the old levels, and the government starts reducing interest rates or increasing budget deficits to increase employment, inflation may emerge before full employment has been re-established. In these circumstances, full employment would only be possible if major parts of the community accepted lower standards of living than they had previously enjoyed.

And what of the second constraint on increasing government borrowing? Budget deficits are funded by borrowing from citizens or foreigners, or by printing money. If the amount of money printing is small, it may not incur a cost to the budget. Rising incomes will increase the amount of money that citizens are happy to hold. But if there is a substantial amount of borrowing from the central bank, beyond some point it will be necessary for the authorities to 'soak up' surplus money, otherwise the abundance of cash will be a source of excess expenditure and inflation. Inflation is, of course, the last thing on anyone's mind during such a crisis. It is in recovery that it becomes a threat to continued growth, requiring the reduction of budget deficits and higher interest rates. The government or the central bank can remove the future inflationary risks by soaking up the surplus money by issuing bonds, on which interest must be paid.

It is obvious enough that there is a budgetary cost associated with borrowing from foreigners. It may not be so obvious that there are economic costs related to a government borrowing from citizens. When the time comes for repayment, won't the government be able to raise taxation on one set of citizens to repay debt to another set of citizens? How is the country worse off if it has to arrange the transfer of money from one set of citizens to another? The problem is that taxation has an economic cost because it distorts decisions to work, save or undertake one (less taxed) economic activity rather than another (more taxed). The raising of taxation to pay interest on and repay debt will reduce to some extent the productive capacity of the economy. For moderate amounts of debt this is likely to be small in comparison with the waste of productive resources through unemployment. But if structural weaknesses prevent the reduction of unemployment, continued deficits may cause the economic costs of servicing debt to become high.

Policy in the transition from Depression Economics to the restoration of full employment involves three main balancing acts. It requires balancing the levels of expenditure and the productive capacity of the economy. The decisions are easy as long as there is deep recession, high unemployment and prospects for their amelioration through increased expenditure, but become more difficult with recovery.

It also requires striking the right balance between average living standards and average productivity of the economy at full employment. If claims for incomes and services exceed the economy's productive capacity, expansionary policies will lead to inflation and to the end of expansion before full employment has been restored. Balance may require reductions in the real levels of incomes or government services, or increased taxation.

Lastly, good policy requires the right balance between present and future living standards. The more the increase in expenditure is focused on productive investment, and the less the deadweight cost of raising taxation is placed on future generations, the higher will be the future living standards that are consistent with sustainable full employment.

Many Nations

Depression Economics theory was worked out for a single economy that was not closely linked to the rest of the world. The policy problem is more complex in a multi-country world.

The level of global output is the sum of the national parts. If the whole world has underemployed resources, as has been the case since the Great Crash of 2008, expansion anywhere will raise incomes, employment and expenditure everywhere else. A substantial proportion of one country's increased expenditure serves to raise demand for imports of other countries' goods and services. To the extent that one country's expanded expenditure 'leaks' into imports from other countries, there is less stimulation of employment and incomes in the home country. To the extent that there is concerted expansion involving many countries, the 'leakages' will balance out, and each country will get more or less its share of the global stimulus.

For a single country, the extent to which its own expansionary policy raises demand for 'home' or 'non-traded' goods and services, and to which it increases demand for other countries' products, depends on the real exchange rate. The real exchange rate in turn depends on what happens to nominal exchange rates (the rates quoted on the news each night) and on domestic relative to foreign inflation.

Here we run into some complexity. The nominal exchange rate is influenced by many things. One factor is the mix between reduced interest rates and increased budget deficits in the policies that lead to increased expenditure. The more that expansion has come from lower interest rates, and the less from increased deficits, the lower the nominal exchange rate. Countries that do relatively little to increase demand through reduced interest rates are likely to experience a rise in the exchange rate, and to receive a lower proportion of the benefit from their own and other countries' expansion than would otherwise have been expected.

Some influences are not closely connected to the settings of policy. The most powerful of these effects is a tendency for capital to 'fly to quality' in an economic crisis; that is, capital will move to economies thought to be relatively safe. Capital also tends to 'fly from risk' in a recession—the economies of developing and resource exporting countries are especially vulnerable.

The flight to quality and away from risk in the immediate aftermath of the Great Crash meant that, for a while, the United States and Japan received a relatively small benefit from their own and other countries' expansionary policies, while most developing and resource exporting countries received a disproportionately large benefit. These were temporary effects: they were greatest in the final months of 2008 and were winding down by the middle of 2009.

The real exchange rate is also affected by differentials in rates of inflation. Countries can experience a fall in the real exchange rate, and an increase in the benefits they receive from their own and other economies' expansion, if their wages and prices at home fall by exceptionally large amounts in recession. After the Great Crash, this improved the competitiveness of East Asia in general, and China in particular. As workers returned to employment in Chinese cities in 2009 after being retrenched in late 2008, it was common to hear that they were being employed at wage levels up to 20 per cent below the old levels. The downward flexibility of East Asian wages in recession increased their competitiveness. The rigidity of the Australian and some European economies reduced competitiveness in a way that is overlooked by a simple focus on nominal exchange rates.

Countries that increase domestic demand the most, and whose real exchange rates fall, tend to recover most rapidly from recession. Global imbalances will be affected by who does the expanding and by changes in real exchange rates. Countries that expand the most and have relatively strong real exchange rates are likely to experience large increases in external payments deficits in the course of recovery. Countries that do little and have relatively weak real exchange rates will tend towards payments surpluses.

The collapse of the old pattern of capital movements through the banks continues to hold imbalances below their boom-time levels, despite what is happening to expenditure and exchange rates. If a deficit cannot be financed, it will not happen. Thus, if a country is experiencing a tendency towards payments deficit, and this cannot be financed by capital inflow, the exchange rate will fall. This will raise net exports and reduce the deficit in current external payments.

The Great Crash and the onset of the Great Recession have been followed by the largest, most broadly based expansionary policies that the world has ever seen. There has never been an application of Depression Economics that is in any way comparable in scale or geographic reach. There was no equivalent concerted expansion in the 1930s because policymakers did not recognise the need for it. There has been no equivalent in other recessions since then because there has been no comparable global recession that required it.

Because this use of policy is unprecedented, it is to some extent experimental. Judgements about its success and its costs in the period ahead will profoundly influence thought about economic policy.

The Great Expansion

The global expansion at first took the form of a rapid reduction of interest rates to near-zero levels in most developed countries. Rates did not go so low in Australia. One of the reasons for this, according to the Governor of the Reserve Bank of Australia, was that Australia's downturn was not as deep as in other countries.[5] Caution about low interest rates introducing new tiers of risk into future financial market behaviour contributed to caution on monetary policy.

Interest rate reductions in many countries were followed by a series of expansionary changes in fiscal policy. By the second quarter of 2009, the developed countries' fiscal expansion had amounted to several per cent of their output stretched over several years, with its greatest concentration in 2010. The earliest and largest fiscal expansions were in China, Korea and Australia. By not taking interest rates down as far as others, Australia chose, by default if not consciously, to rely more on expansionary fiscal policy.

The Australian expansion came in three tranches: in October 2008, February 2009 and May 2009. The first focused on cash payments to low- and medium-income households, and on a large cash grant to first-home buyers. The central features of the second were another cash payment, a large-scale program that subsidised energy-saving private investments in housing insulation, and a similarly large program of school construction. The third tranche, delivered within the annual Budget, confirmed promises of broadly based tax cuts made in more prosperous times, made major commitments to large-scale transport and communications infrastructure, and introduced new support for the commercialisation of new technologies to reduce greenhouse gas emissions in the energy sector. The Australian approach emphasised small-scale and especially housing-related construction. It had the effect of quickly boosting the low end of the housing market and construction activity. Time will tell whether this focus had the effect of perpetuating housing-related distortions from the boom.

The largest, most effective and most influential expansion was in China, where there has been massive fiscal and even larger monetary expansion. In addition, a series of 'industry policy' initiatives has had a substantial stimulatory effect. While international attention has mainly been focused on the set-piece policy announcement of November 2008, the reality has been embodied in a series of actions. University of California economist Barry Naughton has estimated the first-year stimulatory effect of fiscal measures at about 3 per cent of GDP, alongside monetary expansion contributing about 10 per cent of GDP.[6] The fiscal and monetary elements were at first heavily focused on increased investment, especially in infrastructure, although there were subsidies for the purchase of consumer durables from the beginning.

The effects of the expansionary policy were soon apparent. In January 2009, our assessment, provided to the Prime Minister of Australia, was that Chinese growth through the year, from the December quarter of 2008 to the same quarter of 2009, was likely to be in the range of 10 to 12 per cent. Subsequent information has confirmed that judgement.

One consequence of the domestic expenditure expansion was that imports fell proportionately much less rapidly than exports. The higher base of exports meant that this did not immediately translate into a lower trade surplus. By May 2009, the surplus seemed to be stabilising after years of expansion. It can be expected to fall later in 2009 and into 2010. The stabilisation and then growth of Chinese imports will be an important source of support for global recovery.

The global expansionary policies so far can be judged another successful application of Depression Economics, following the brilliant success of the large risks taken by China in the Asian Financial Crisis. By the second quarter of 2009, Chinese output was growing at the high rates of the years before the Great Crash. Australian output, meanwhile, stopped falling in the first quarter of 2009. Output in the developed countries was expected to stabilise later in 2009, and to grow weakly through 2010.

But not all countries and regions are doing well. For some, there is the question of whether the stimulatory policies have gone far enough. Separately, for many countries, bailout policies leave the vulnerabilities that contributed to the Great Crash in place.

The uneven application of expansionary policies across countries, plus changes in real exchange rates, are causing uneven effects on global imbalances. Overall imbalances have become substantially smaller. They will become smaller yet, at least until the memories of 2008 recede. It seems likely that the end of the recession will see smaller surpluses in East Asia. Europe, having been more cautious with fiscal expansion, is likely to loom larger in the world's surplus countries. The Anglosphere's continued capacity to borrow on government account, and the weak commitment to redress domestic imbalances, will keep it in deficit, but at lower levels than before the Crash.

Part III
Aftermath

10

Growth after the Rampage

THE HARVARD-BASED JAPAN scholar Edwin Reischauer records in his autobiography the difficulty we all have in accepting major changes in an established economic order. From time to time in the years after World War II he would revise his book *The United States and Japan*, and each time he would be condemned by reviewers for being over-optimistic. And yet each time he would be forced by the evidence to be more positive than he had been the time before. Again he would be condemned. This was a great puzzle to the man who later would be Kennedy's ambassador to Japan. Then the penny dropped. It was much more acceptable to be pessimistic about change and wrong, than optimistic and right.[1]

So it has been with the economic success of all of the latecomers to development. The phenomenon of rapid growth through 'catching up' with others is a natural process. Once it begins there are powerful tendencies to keep going. Something way out of the ordinary is required to stop it. And if it keeps going for long enough in a country with a big population, it changes the global political order as well as the economic order. And yet we are all slow to recognise the significance of what is happening.

China has more than ten times the population of Japan. Huge changes in the global power structure were being ground out by the growth of China when America was apparently doing well. After the Great Crash and its hobbling of the old industrial countries, the pace of change will be noticeable even to the dull human eye.

This is the distinctive impact of the Crash: an acceleration of ongoing trends. It is likely that the world economy will return to strong growth, at rates not far below the exceptional levels of the early years of the twenty-first century. But the distribution of that growth will be radically different. It will be heavily concentrated in the successful developing countries, particularly the biggest three—China, India and Indonesia.

One, Two, Three: You're Out

The ramifications of the Crash in a particular country are dependent on whether that country 'strikes out' on each of three issues. The first is the extent to which a country provided a home to the global financial institutions that suffered large losses. The Crash will be a heavy drag on growth in those countries whose domestic banking systems have been most affected, and which have carried the heaviest load of bailing out failed banks.

The second is the size of the external payments deficits with which a country entered the crisis. The most export-oriented economies, and those with large external trade and payments surpluses, were hit harder by the Crash when it happened. The countries with large trade and payments deficits will take longer to recover.

The third issue is the extent to which a country specialised in commodity exports and therefore suffered a decline following the Crash in its export prices and terms of trade.

On the first strike, the home countries of the failed financial institutions now face several challenges. The destruction of the domestic system of financial inter-mediation, as well as the reduction of gains from the division of labour, have gone much further in these places. This is simply because the failed institutions have proportionately much larger roles at home. In addition, the responsibility for bailing them out falls on their own governments; the costs of raising taxation to recoup some of the immense losses are all theirs.

It was an advantage for a country to be home to conservative (even backward) banks and other financial institutions. The nationally owned banks of some countries, including China, South Africa, India, Canada and Indonesia, were little touched by the excesses of Clever Money and the problems revealed by the Great Crash. Overseas financial firms damaged by the Crash had taken substantial equity positions in all major Chinese banks in the early twenty-first century. But the doubtful practices of the foreign partners were not introduced on a large scale. Perhaps it was only a matter of timing, and China was lucky that the influence of its new foreign partners was in its early stages.

There are also many cases of conservative banks with domestic owners doing reasonably well in small developing countries. One such example is Papua New Guinea, which has a nationally owned private bank, the Bank of South Pacific, that accounts for nearly half of the country's banking business. On the whole, however, small and poorly performing developing countries were heavily reliant on foreign banks for international and many domestic transactions, and suffered severely from the collapse of the global financial firms.

The incidence of the fiscal burden of bailing out failed banks has fallen unevenly across countries. The collapse of the large and venerable Netherlands bank ABN AMRO and its absorption by the British bank HBOS meant that the British taxpayer carried the consequences of the failures of Dutch bankers and regulators. American taxpayers ended up carrying the full costs of the losses in other countries of the financial institutions that called the United States home. These included the immense losses of the London-based rogue subsidiary of the American Insurance Group.

The second strike requires some explanation. Savings in excess of investment in some countries, and shortfalls of savings in others, raise the welfare of surplus and deficit countries alike. Losses are suffered by both when they are forced by external events to tailor domestic expenditure more closely to the current value of production of their own economies.

We have noted how the initial shock of the Great Crash fell more heavily on the surplus countries.

However, afterwards, the task of adjusting expenditure to production became more difficult in the deficit countries. The government of the deficit country has to induce lower levels of expenditure. It has to reduce either or, more likely, both consumption and investment. It has to implement policies that will secure this result: higher interest rates; higher taxation; lower government expenditure. The surplus country has the inherently easier task of encouraging higher consumption and investment.

The challenge of adjustment in the deficit country may be temporarily postponed to the extent that it still has access to international capital markets. Access to such capital shrank drastically with the Great Crash. The United States, as the home of the world's reserve currency, for the time being continues to have exceptional advantages in borrowing abroad. And countries with strong credit ratings, such as most of the developed countries, including Australia, could borrow on official accounts even when private markets had shrivelled. But the postponement of adjustment leads to larger costs when the time comes to face it.

The power of the third strike depends considerably on the policy that was in place before the Crash. Commodity exporters experienced an unprecedented increase in their terms of trade in the five years preceding the crisis, but their export prices fell sharply in the second half of 2008. The exceptional growth of the large developing countries drove up commodity prices in the boom. These economies are at a stage of development at which economic growth uses resources intensively, and markets had been taken by surprise by the strength of demand. This led to prices temporarily rising well above what would be needed to induce adequate supplies of minerals, energy, food and agricultural raw materials in the long term, even with the continuation of Platinum Age growth. However, the disruption of strong growth in the large developing countries, and the crashes in the developed economies, caused average export prices for commodities to fall.

The strike is heavier for countries that spent the proceeds of high terms of trade during the boom, and raised domestic expenditure to levels that were not sustainable in normal times. Major importers of commodities are assisted in the restoration of prosperity by the improvement in terms of trade that follows the Crash.

Some countries had no strikes against them, China and India among them. Members of the Anglosphere mostly have two strikes against them. Most commodity exporting countries had at least one strike against them, but not necessarily if they had avoided increasing expenditure excessively at the height of the boom.

Economic circumstances can obviously be made better or worse by how they are managed by government. The easy days of economic policy are those when the community's expectations of expenditure are below the economy's productive capacity, augmented as it may be by the sensible and sustainable use of international funding. The difficult days of policy are those during which expectations of expenditure exceed the productive capacity of the economy.[2]

In places and times in which expectations of incomes and expenditure fit comfortably within a country's capacity to produce goods and services, it will be easier to run policies to secure full employment and price stability. These are circumstances that are conducive to high rates of investment and productivity growth, which further increase the expenditure and incomes that are consistent with economic stability and full employment in the future.

On the other hand, during the difficult days, the lowering of expectations and expenditure to sustainable levels creates immense political strain. To the extent that the task is for the time being beyond the will or capacity of the polity, economic instability and distortions in resource allocation reduce the productive capacity of the economy even more. Countries that find themselves in the difficult days of economic policy are more likely to make policy mistakes that compound the difficulties.

Other Factors

Countries had widely different capacities for economic growth independently of the crisis. Countries experiencing strong economic growth in the 'catching up' stage of development have inherent advantages. So do countries that for other reasons are experiencing exceptionally strong productivity growth, or have recently undergone experiences that reduce the community's expectations about expenditure.

There are some common challenges across all countries during the recovery from financial crisis and recession. Countries will face better future prospects the more that expansionary recovery policies increase the productive capacity of the economy. Policies that favour investment over consumption, and also the growth of productivity, have favourable consequences. Policies that merely encourage consumption do not.

Global economic growth will be affected by the fragility of the international financial system after the Crash. There will be fewer and weaker large international banks. They will be more cautious about lending to 'risky' developing countries and more generally about funding 'risky' activities, notwithstanding the irony that the weaknesses in the crisis were centred in the main financial businesses in the main developed countries. This will matter a great deal in the home countries of the badly damaged banks and for international capital flows.

In the best of circumstances, the world will have lost for a considerable period much of the good that came from the use of clever new products. It will have lost some of the capacity to hedge foreign exchange and commodity price risks, and willingness to take risks in investment and trade. This will reduce to some extent the rate of productive innovation in the global economy, as entrepreneurs lose some sources of finance for risky projects. But a diminished role for innovative finance would also reduce vulnerability to the recurrence of financial crisis. There would be net gains from reduced use of the financial innovations of the late twentieth and early twenty-first centuries. Better still would be efficient regulation that allowed limited, productive use of the new instruments without increasing the exposure to crisis.

There are some other ways in which the legacies of the Great Crash and Great Recession could have negative effects on future productivity growth. The most important of these is the possibility that there will be a general mistrust of markets, and a tendency for governments to intervene inappropriately in the allocation of resources within economies.

One clear lesson of the Crash is that the financial markets, understood broadly to include the markets for equities traded in these markets, requires much more close, effective and carefully thought out and designed regulation than became the practice in the United States over the past decade. The challenge is to build the political case for more effective regulation of finance without opening the door to economically damaging intervention in other markets.

Lower growth in one part of the world will obviously lower total global growth. So poor economic management in one country lowers global output, even after the deficiency in aggregate demand has been corrected. It also decreases the opportunities for incomes growth in other countries by reducing their opportunities for trade and specialisation.

High-income Industrial Economies

The immediate effects of the collapse of the financial conglomerates and the need suddenly to reduce the imbalances were first felt most powerfully in the economies with particularly large surpluses and trade shares of output. All high-income surplus countries were severely affected—Japan, Germany, Singapore, Hong Kong and Korea among them.

The initial contraction was more severe in the high-income surplus economies partly because they lacked the growth momentum of China and the other Asian developing countries. Japan in particular also lacked the structural flexibility of these countries, with the sclerosis of an ageing population being more advanced. The concentration of their exports in high-quality, expensive variations of products made them more vulnerable to the choices of consumers and producers as recession reduced purchasing power.

Japan was saved from the worst problems of the financial institutions partly by weakness and caution in its banks following the crash of the early 1990s. They had suffered prolonged trauma as they sought to restore profitability and the integrity of their balance sheets while postponing the declaration of the true market value of large amounts of non-performing assets.[3]

While all countries were damaged by the fall of the American and European financial institutions, the regulatory and fiscal responsibility for correcting the problems was left by default with the home governments. The large countries felt that their major financial institutions were too big to fail; for the smaller countries, they were sometimes too big to rescue. The treasuries of some large developed countries, notably the United States and the United Kingdom, have been left with immense public debt from the bailouts, the servicing of which is likely to contribute to a long period of tepid growth. Resentment will grow in the countries funding the large bailouts as the long-term constraints on living standards are recognised. National political behaviour will be affected for a long time by this damaging episode, in ways that are unpredictable in detail but deeply problematic.

All of the major developed economies experienced large initial gains from the effects of recession on the terms of trade. High prices for oil and other commodities had diminished incomes in the later stages of the boom. A high proportion of the loss was regained over a short period, as energy, minerals and food prices fell sharply in the second half of 2008.

How will the varying approaches to bank refinancing and remediation, and fiscal and monetary expansion, interact with other factors to shape recovery in the main three developed regions?

The underlying capacity to sustain economic growth is stronger in the United States than in the two other major developed regions. This is due to higher levels of immigration, faster population growth and the slower ageing of the population, as well as a less-restrained market economy. These inherent advantages of the United States in combination with the early, immense fiscal and monetary expansion will generate early impulses to recovery.

Of the major developed regions, the United States and the United Kingdom were large deficit countries prior to the crisis. The contraction of the global imbalances will significantly reduce their capacity for growth during the considerable period of adjustment to diminished capital inflow. Japan and to a lesser extent Germany and some other continental European economies face the opposite adjustment: to higher domestic expenditure.

Overall, it seems likely that US growth will lack its accustomed exuberance for a long period as it covers the immense costs of bailing out failed financial institutions, and also changes the focus of consumers towards greater savings and the orientation of the economy towards greater investment and exports. European growth will be slower, and when recovery comes it will be similarly burdened by the costs of servicing the debts incurred to bail out financial institutions. The United Kingdom will be particularly disadvantaged because of its external deficits prior to the crisis.

Japan alone of the large developed countries has no strikes against it. Despite the greater initial depth of its recession, it may recover earlier levels of growth relatively quickly, supported by exports to neighbouring China. For Japan, this means a return to slow growth—perhaps little different to the tepid growth in the United States and Europe.

One wild card in the aftermath of the crisis is whether the US dollar will retain its status as the world's overwhelmingly dominant reserve and transactions currency. This status lowers the cost of US official and private borrowing. It supports large external debt and current account deficits in prosperity and recession. But since the Great Crash, there have been expressions of anxiety from the East Asian surplus countries about the value of US dollar-denominated assets in future. The Chinese Premier in April 2009 floated the idea that the dollar's reserve currency role should be shared by a synthetic international currency, but then played down the suggestion.

The initial global response to the Great Crash was to strengthen the role of the dollar. Capital flooded into it and the yen because they were seen as 'safe havens' in uncertain times. The dollar strengthened for a while, running against US authorities' efforts to stimulate demand for domestic goods and services.

The easing of panic in the financial markets has allowed a cooler look at the dollar, though it is unlikely that international political action will develop a credible alternative reserve currency. The historic power of US capital markets to attract global savings has relied in large measure on the transparency arising from its clear rules about risk and reward, ownership and bankruptcy. The growth of the shadow banking system, and the absence of regulation, involved a systematic departure from those rules. This introduces unfamiliar risks.

It is possible that a combination of continued dollar depreciation and decline in the United States' proportionate role in international transactions will lead to the use of other currencies alongside the dollar. This would increase the cost of financing US debt, and force the more rapid reduction of the United States' external deficit.

An early and rapid diversification of global reserve assets would be painful for the United States. But if diversification were to occur, it is important that the adjustments occur within disciplined American expenditure policies designed to accommodate it. The British experience with the pound sterling over half a century from World War I demonstrates the costs of a slow decommissioning of a reserve currency in the absence of supportive domestic expenditure policies.

Asian Developing Economies

As we have said, the three strikes together work in favour of Asian developing countries. These have substantial domestic financial institutions that were not major participants in the financial innovation and excess that led to the boom and the bust. They went into the Crash with large external surpluses. They have mostly experienced increases in their terms of trade as commodity prices have fallen.

The Great Crash and Great Recession came in favourable political circumstances for the large, successful Asian developing countries. In October 2008, the Chinese leadership was experienced and tested, one year into a second five-year term. Taiwan saw a change in leadership that was highly favourable for management of the difficult issues across the Straits. General elections in both Indonesia and India in 2009 strengthened the positions of leaders with good records in economic policy.

The industrialising Asian economies suffered immediate and immense contraction of exports as the major developed countries fell into recession. In China, this coincided with the first 'market-based' contraction in commercial real estate and a large fall in the value of assets traded on local stock exchanges. These developments together triggered the sharp destocking of a wide range of final products and industrial inputs, exacerbating the contraction. However, the improvement in China's terms of trade was considerable in the second half of 2008. China is such a large country that its own rapid growth now reduces its export prices and raises its import prices.

Its recovery has been turning the terms of trade against itself again in early 2009, although not back to anywhere near the unfavourable levels of the boom.

Following the initial hit, China's position was relatively favourable on every measure. Its prime policy challenge was to secure a huge increase in domestic expenditure. Consumption or investment by the private or government sector was needed to fill the gap left by the collapse in external demand and compounded by the turn in the real estate cycle. It had the capacity for large fiscal and monetary expansion, on account of its sound fiscal and unparalleled external payments position.

The shift to growth from domestic expenditure expansion requires swift, large and determined change in policy, and is administratively demanding. China was able to work through financial institutions relatively unburdened by bad assets left over from the boom.

The Chinese economic response to the Great Crash was spectacular. The negative inventory cycle ran its course by January 2009 in some industries, and by February or March in others. Investment by firms with connections to all levels of government grew immediately and strongly, facilitated by projects left over from a long period of anti-inflationary constraint. The growth rate stabilised late in the first quarter of 2009, with growth in the year to the March quarter down to 6.1 per cent. It then began to accelerate. Workers from rural areas began to move back to the big industrial cities. An official survey suggests that after Spring Festival 2009, about 56 million of the 70 million who had made the move back to their villages had returned to the cities and 45 million were in jobs.[4]

The strong, domestic-oriented growth in China's output is bound to reduce its external trade and payments surplus. The powerful growth in its imports is the first stimulus to global trade expansion after the slump. China has also played a role in holding up foreign direct investment (FDI) on a global scale. World FDI fell by more than 20 per cent in 2008 and has been heading lower still in 2009. Inflows into China, excluding the financial sector, doubled in 2008, but were falling late in the year.[5]

China's demand and import growth will have the largest stimulatory effect in the western Pacific economies and in the commodity exporting countries. By April 2009 it was already contributing to restoration of export growth in its immediate neighbours.

There was some counterbalancing pressure from increased Chinese competitiveness in labour-intensive products, which affected countries competing directly in these areas, including India, Indonesia and Vietnam. The easing of Chinese growth ended for a while the rising labour costs that had been making Chinese producers less competitive in export markets for simple, labour-intensive manufactures, and forcing them towards more capital-intensive and technologically sophisticated products. It therefore temporarily delayed the expansion of export opportunity in other labour-abundant economies that were behind China in levels of development. For them, this will have slowed growth for a while. But only for a while.

By contrast, Asian developing economies that were a step or two ahead of China in the growth process and had higher incomes, and also the resource exporting countries, have been unambiguously helped by the swift structural change that has preserved Chinese competitiveness and supported the return to rapid growth. Malaysia, Thailand and perhaps the Philippines are among these countries.

More generally, the tendencies towards reductions in China's trade and payments surplus through rapid expansion of domestic demand and imports will increase net exports of China's trading partners all over the world.

Commodity Exporting Countries

The commodity exporting countries comprise several groups of countries. There are a few high-income econo-mies: Australia, Norway, New Zealand and to a lesser extent Canada. There are the specialised petroleum exporters, such as the Organisation of the Petroleum Exporting Countries (OPEC) and Russia. There are other developing countries, including many with low incomes, weak domestic governance and poor recent experience of and prospects for economic growth.

Recession in the Platinum Age uses resources more intensively than recession in earlier periods. This became more obvious when Chinese growth began to recover from the first shocks of the Great Crash.

The commodity exporting countries suffered imme-diately and severely from the Great Crash. The collapse of international financial intermediation and the contrac-tion in trade volumes and commodity prices with which it was associated had a large and immediate effect on export volumes and values. The currency adjustments assisted efforts in the resource exporting countries to reduce real expenditure and to increase incentives to produce tradeable rather than non-tradeable goods and services.

The economic consequences of global recession depend on how economies had used the increased incomes generated by the preceding boom conditions. Countries that had limited domestic demand expansion and run a correspondingly large payments surplus during the resources boom are in reasonably sound positions. Countries that had increased domestic expenditure to the expanded limits of the boom times have to reduce expenditure by large amounts, at great difficulty and cost in the aftermath of the Crash.

Australia is an interesting case of a commodity exporting country. The Great Crash followed seventeen years of continuous expansion, at an average rate faster than in any other Organisation for Economic Co-operation and Development country. For the first ten years, to about 2001, this was based upon productivity growth from economic reform. The end of the productivity boom was followed by several years of housing and consumption boom, and from about 2004, the China-led resources boom. The period of rising incomes without productivity growth underwrote what has been described as the 'Great Australian Complacency of the Early Twenty-First Century', when economic reform and discipline came to be considered incidental to prosperity.[6]

Australia ran modest Budget surpluses at the height of the boom, although smaller as a proportion of GDP than many resource exporting countries. Australian

Treasury calculations indicate that an overwhelming proportion of the huge increase in federal government revenues through the resources boom were spent as they arrived, as increased public expenditure or tax cuts.[7] The Budget (abstracting from cyclical influences) went into substantial structural deficit in 2006–07. Australia ran immodest current account deficits.

Despite the lift in export prices from 2003 to 2008 adding around two-thirds to export income and more than one sixth to total incomes, Australia's current account deficit rose to even higher levels, to 7.4 per cent of GDP, its peak in the March quarter of 2008.[8] The ubiquitous housing and consumption boom early in the century reduced household savings to below zero. As we have seen, the increase in expenditure on housing and consumption was funded mainly by borrowing from overseas banks. The growth in corporate borrowing funded a substantial increase in investment. Negative private saving overwhelmed a small increase in government savings. The encouragement of consumption and housing in the first years of the new century was one of several factors that kept productivity growth below the 1990s.

Australia has two strikes against it: its huge current account deficits before the crisis, and the deterioration in its terms of trade. They mean that Australia will have to reduce average consumption levels more than most countries if it is to restore full employment on a sustainable basis.

Australian authorities embarked on the fastest and one of the largest stimulatory responses of the high-income countries. This has limited the early loss of production, employment and incomes. The stimulus was assisted by the sharp fall of the Australian dollar, until it was considerably reversed through the first half of 2009.

But there are hard times ahead. Sustainable full employment will require reduction of average incomes and living standards below those to which Australians became accustomed before the Crash. The Australian Government, community and business leadership has barely begun to contemplate the adjustment that is required. There is a danger that the lack of awareness of the hard realities will lead to poor management of the difficult days of economic policy.

Beyond Australia, most resource exporting countries did not raise expenditure so far towards the temporarily higher limits of the boom. For them, the adjustment will be less demanding.

The continuation of strong growth in the large developing countries is likely to keep global prices for minerals and energy well above the levels of the late twentieth century. Most agricultural products will continue the price increases of the early twenty-first century, reversing what had been a long-term deterioration in relative prices.

Those commodity exporting countries that managed to save a large part of the exceptional income from the commodity price boom will now do reasonably well. There will still be fluctuations in commodity prices around a higher average. However, the exceptionally high prices immediately preceding the Great Crash are unlikely to re-turn soon except in brief and exceptional episodes.

The Poorest Countries

The poorest countries, weakly linked to the global trading and financial systems, might be thought to be little exposed to the Great Crash and global recession. Alas, this is not the case. They are much more dependent on external aid than other developing countries, and the real value of aid has fallen during the crisis. Although levels of trade and direct foreign investment in the poorest countries are low, they receive large benefits from them. Investors' unwillingness to accept risk in crisis hurts trade and investment in the poorest countries much more than others.

There had been momentum in the early twenty-first century for special international measures to accelerate development in the poorest countries. The United Nations announced ambitious 'millennium goals' for the reduction of poverty requiring large increases in development assistance. For a while before the Great Crash, development outcomes were consistent with the goals. The gains included unprecedented strong economic growth in Africa.

The big increases in commodity prices towards the end of the Platinum Age boom provided opportunities for the acceleration of incomes growth in many developing countries. For some, however, high food and energy prices meant a deterioration in national terms of trade. They also represented an increase in the cost of living, and lower living standards for poor people.[9] After the large increase in food prices in early 2008, World Bank President Bob Zoellick announced his intention to lead an effort to double the funding for international agricultural research, which is recognised as being especially important and valuable in low-income countries.

These various initiatives have been downgraded or abandoned in recession. The large increase in funding for the International Monetary Fund at the Group of 20 leaders' meeting in London in April 2009 was mainly to support developing countries through the financial crisis. The G8 meeting in Italy in July 2009 was the occasion for strong rhetorical re-commitment to increased development assistance. Let's wait and see.

Growth in the poorest economies has been affected in the early stages of global recession. The effects of the crisis are likely to be protracted. Increased aid and direct foreign investment from China have been considerable, but alone cannot meet the requirements of continued growth in the low-income developing countries. In the absence of a change in approach to development assistance from the developed countries, the poorest countries are likely to be the biggest victims of the Great Crash of 2008.

11

The Elephant's Footprints

GEORGE III'S ENVOY ARRIVED at the court of the Manchu emperor in Beijing in September 1793. Britain was in the first decades of the industrial revolution, and China was the world's biggest economy and strongest state. Earl George McCartney explained to the Son of Heaven the many advantages of close trade and diplomatic relations with newly industrialising Britain. It had been an awkward start because McCartney had refused the traditional 'kowtow'. Emperor Qianlong did not stand forever on dignity, and considered the matter. He later delivered his verdict: the Chinese empire had no need of the things that were made in Britain.

Less than half a century later, after an exhausting debate in the House of Commons, British warships sank the Chinese fleet at Canton and supervised the raising of the Union Jack over Hong Kong, to make the China coast safe for opium from India.

Earlier cooperation may have had some benefit for China after all.

The taking root in China of the productive plants of the industrial revolution is changing the power relations again. The changes have accelerated with the Great Crash. But one thing that has not changed at all is the value of close understanding and cooperation between old and new powers.

The Great Crash of 2008 is the first global financial crisis in the time of globalisation. It has increased the importance and the difficulty of effective international cooperation to avoid threats to order and prosperity.

The long period of bipolar strategic balance during the Cold War was followed by a brief, promising, but ultimately turbulent 'unipolar moment', from the collapse of the Soviet Union to the failure of the most recent war in Iraq. The inexorable economic growth of China and India means that the unipolar moment will eventually be followed by a quadripolar structure. The United States and a more deeply integrated European Union will be joined sooner than had been anticipated by China and India as the entities whose economic and strategic weights far exceed those of the next rung of powers: Japan, Russia, Indonesia and Brazil.

In a quadripolar world, the support or acquiescence of the four big entities will be required for any effective international action. The constitutions of international organisations will need to be revised to accommodate the new power realities. For example, India will need to be a permanent member of the United Nations (UN) Security Council, and Europe will need to be represented singularly as the European Union. International organisations seeking to play a role in the coordination of world affairs will need to be open to the four large powers: the Group of 20 (G20) has a chance and the Group of Eight (G8) does not. The relationship between the United States and China will be at the core of this world.

The Great Crash does not fundamentally change these geostrategic tectonic shifts. It does, however, accelerate movement towards the new balance. There is a danger that the movement will now be too fast for the intellectual and political elites of the four great powers of the future, and for the rest of us, to think and work through the implications of the emerging international order.

Economic tsunamis are associated with tectonic movements. They mark the transition from one state of international power relations to another. The rapid emergence of the modern industrial economy in Britain in the late eighteenth century, and then in other parts of the north Atlantic, laid the foundations for the era of imperialism. More abruptly, it was the growth of British debt to fund World War I that shifted the centre of global power from London to New York and Washington within a few years from 1918. Britain's long stagnation as it worked off the economic legacy of war, and then the economic shock of another war, marked the end of European imperialism and the emergence of the bipolar world of the Cold War.

The Great Crash brings forward in time the quadripolar power structure primarily through a premature, relative weakening of the two established economic powers: the United States and the European Union. It therefore leads the world prematurely into the transition. The quadripolar realities are weakly formed. During the transition several states, including Japan, will have claims and many others will stake claims for veto powers over international actions affecting their interests.

Despite the difficulties, close and effective international cooperation in this period will be needed to moderate the threat of war between states; to support development in the poorest countries and avoid the manifold risks of state failure; to maintain global economic stability; to mitigate the risk of dangerous human-induced climate change; and to regulate trade and financial transactions in an increasingly global economy.

Geopolitical Shifts and Peace

The influence of a country on the organisation of international society depends partly but not only on economic size. This is mediated by technological capacity, the priority given to military and strategic goals, and the diplomatic capability to manage alliances, friendships and enmities.

A country makes implicit or explicit choices about the time in history when it exercises military authority. High military expenditure enhances a country's power for the present, but weakens a country economically and therefore also weakens its future military capability. The former Soviet Union temporarily exercised power out of proportion to its economic weight in the 1970s and 1980s. The strain that this placed on its economy led to a comprehensive decline in its strategic weight.

By contrast the large reductions in military expenditure in the United States after the Cold War strengthened the country's budgetary position and lowered the cost of capital for productive economic investment. By the end of the Clinton presidency in 2000, the United States had enhanced its strategic primacy in world affairs. Under the presidency of George W Bush, however, these processes went into reverse. The high priority of military expenditure was part of the cause of the external payments weakness that was an organ of the Great Crash elephant.

Joseph Nye of Harvard University has drawn attention to the importance of exercising 'soft power', or the capacity to influence others by the attractiveness of one's own culture and society. More recently he has discussed 'smart power'—the capacity to integrate the use of military and soft power.[1] Clearly, economic size also helps the exercising of 'soft' power.

The gap between growth rates in the established industrial countries, and China and other large developing countries, will grow wider during the recovery from crisis. China, India and Indonesia will 'catch up' at a faster rate. If the emerging quadripolar world with its bipolar core is to manage associated changes in power realities, it must accelerate the reform of some international institutions and the development of new ones.

The new approaches will require greater international support for the United States in the maintenance of international order. They will also require US acceptance of greater consultation and the sharing of influence that will accompany greater international burden sharing.

The new economic powers will need to accept leadership roles to which they are unaccustomed.

These are difficult requirements. For a while at least, we will live in a riskier world.

Bipolar Cooperation for Economic Stability

The maintenance of global economic stability and growth is among the issues that can no longer be solved without cooperation between China and the United States.

It is clear that there were risks in early twenty-first century imbalances for surplus and deficit countries. China could have set out to reduce its surplus by increasing domestic expenditure. To avoid unwelcome inflationary pressures (and inflation had emerged as an issue immediately before the Crash), it would have had to raise the foreign exchange value of the yuan earlier and more than it did. Alternatively, it could have ignored the inflation risk and held the yuan steady while increasing expenditure. This would have led to higher inflation within China which, in turn, would have raised the real (inflation-adjusted) exchange rate, slowed export growth and raised imports. Regardless of how the increase in the real exchange rate were achieved, exports would have grown more slowly and imports more rapidly.

An increase in expenditure is easier said than done, at least if it is to be useful in raising current and future standards of living. There is a limited capacity to plan and implement efficient government programs. The household consumer is not so easily persuaded over a short period that her interests are served more by increased consumption than increased savings. That said, the early success of the Chinese Government in quickly increasing domestic expenditure after the Great Crash of 2008 suggests that more could have been done earlier. It is notable that the rapid expenditure increases since October 2008 have been dominated by investment.

If it had been possible to substantially increase expenditure in China before the Great Crash, we cannot be entirely sure whether this would have led to lower, similar or higher growth rates than were actually achieved. The increase would probably have been focused mainly on investment, broadly defined to include education and other avenues to the improvement of the productive capacity of the labour force. It's a shocking thought that this would have generated an even higher rate of growth.

The rising real exchange rate would have forced the accelerated restructuring of the export and import-competing sectors of the economy. Labour-intensive production would have declined more rapidly, and the emergence of newly competitive and more technologically sophisticated, capital-intensive production would have been more rapid. The maintenance of high employment and a socially acceptable distribution of income would depend heavily on the composition of the expansion of government expenditure.

If China had adopted such an alternative strategy before the Crash, the crisis would have been less costly for it and its international partners.

The United States would have faced unpalatable choices. There would have been a more challenging inflation environment, one in which the funding of private and public deficits was more difficult and costly. Interest rates and taxation would have had to be higher and government expenditure lower. President George W Bush's wars would have been contested more strongly on economic grounds. Economic growth, incomes and employment would have been lower than they were. But through these means, the US deficit would have fallen more or less commensurately with the Chinese surplus. The United States would have been less vulnerable to the Great Crash.

What if the United States had not been prepared to do these hard things in response to Chinese adjustment? The result would have been higher global inflation and interest rates, and probably greater vulnerability to financial instability. This would have been a bad outcome for China, the United States and the world as a whole.

On the other hand, what if the United States had heeded the warning signs in external deficits before the Great Crash, and alone had tried to take preventive action? Could it have unilaterally taken steps to reduce its deficits, thereby forcing China to accept lower surpluses? If the US Government had been less profligate with expenditure or tax cuts, and had run much lower budget deficits in the George W Bush era, this would have lowered the exchange rate (and also long-term interest rates). Export growth would have been stronger and import growth weaker. This would have fed back into smaller Chinese exports and larger imports. China's external surplus would have been lower. In the absence of countervailing increases in Chinese expenditure, growth would have been lower in both China and the United States. Unilateral and unreciprocated action along these lines would not have been an attractive option.

The best result would have been active coordination of macro-economic policy, within which increased expenditure in China coincided with expenditure restraint in the United States. Cooperation would have created less risky and more rewarding policy options for both countries.

Restoring Development in a World of Poverty

Until the Great Crash, the Platinum Age provided a favourable environment for development everywhere. While the large developing countries have been able to quickly restore strong growth momentum after the Great Crash, the poorer developing countries have not.

A global effort to strengthen and enlarge international public mechanisms for channelling development resources to poor developing countries could make a substantial difference, including to the effectiveness of new Chinese funding. The G20 commitments in April 2009 to reform and expand the resources of the International Monetary Fund and the World Bank laid a foundation upon which substantial measures could be built. But there have been few signs of an effective follow-up.

In the absence of much larger global development assistance flows, the Great Crash may come to mark a divide between an early twenty-first century period when global growth was more broadly based than ever before, and one when growth was concentrated in more advanced developing countries.

Apart from its immense humanitarian significance, failure of development in poorer countries will increase the chances of state failure, and with it demands on international security cooperation.

The developed world may come to regret the neglect of the development consequences of the Great Crash.

Climate Change Policy

The Great Crash descended on the world economy at a crucial time for the mitigation of human-induced global warming. Time is running out for effective action to be taken to avoid dangerous climate change.[2] A conference under UN auspices in Copenhagen in December 2009 will play a crucial role in shaping international action.

The acceleration of economic growth in the early twenty-first century was associated with a lift in the trajectory of greenhouse gas emissions, and the new locus of growth was the large developing countries. These countries were at stages of development in which any increase in economic activity used energy intensively. China, India and Indonesia all happen to be economies in which coal, the most emissions-intensive of major energy sources, is a relatively abundant and cheap local source of energy.

The Platinum Age brought forward the time when greenhouse gas concentrations introduced high risks of dangerous climate change. The challenge of mitigation policy is to transform the relationship between economic output and greenhouse gas emissions, so that global economic growth can proceed without human-induced, dangerous climate change.

Climate change cannot be solved by a single country or a small group of countries. This is a diabolical international policy problem because each country will be better off if it contributes little to global mitigation efforts, so long as its free-riding does not undermine the mitigation efforts of others. The only solution to the free-riding problem is an agreement within which each substantial country agrees to reduce emissions by an appropriate amount as long as others take proportionate action.

What is an appropriate contribution by one country to a global effort to reduce the risks of dangerous climate change? This will be assessed differently by different governments. The challenge is to define an approach to the allocation of a highly constrained emissions budget across countries that all significant countries judge to be acceptable.

The Great Recession following the Great Crash affected the outlook for international action on climate change in three ways. First, it slowed the growth in emissions for a while. Second, it reduced the opportunity cost of investment to introduce low-emissions processes and products. Third, it adversely altered the political environment for new policies requiring difficult structural change.

There was a marked fall in emissions in many countries as the Great Recession struck in one economy after another through 2008: on an early estimate, by 3.3 per cent in the US and 1.5 per cent in the EU for fossil fuels and cement. The increase in the global total was about half that in the preceding years.[3]

But while global emissions stabilised or declined slightly for a time, they still remained well above levels that increased concentrations in the atmosphere. In the absence of mitigation measures, the restoration of strong economic growth in the large developing countries will see emissions growth return to something like the trajectory that it was on before the Crash. The brief cessation of growth due to the recession is likely to delay the arrival of the levels of emissions expected for 2030 by only a few years.

Recovery from recession is a good time economically for structural change. It is a time when the availability of unemployed resources makes investment in new productive capacity relatively cheap. The heavy investment in infrastructure in many countries' recovery programs provides opportunities for accelerating investment in low-emissions goods, services and processes. This opportunity has been taken to varying degrees in the European Union, China, Australia and the United States.

The consequences of the Great Recession for the politics of climate change policy are negative and great. Reduced employment in some activities is felt intensely, while gains in employment in other activities aren't noticed. The 2008 crisis has tended to reinforce the influence of vested interests in the political process in the developed democracies, making strong climate change policies more difficult.

At a crucial time, it seems less likely that individual countries will introduce policies that would add up to effective mitigation, and for the international community to agree on them. But it may not turn out that way. The Great Crash roughly coincided with the departure from office of governments in the United States and Australia that had stood outside international agreements on climate change. The Obama administration in particular has changed the dynamics of international cooperation.

The haunting question raised by the financial crisis is whether a US government that is committed to effective action that damages some corporate interests is free to pursue policies that it judges to be in the national interest. The experience of the European Union and Australia on climate change policy is not reassuring.

Powerful vested interests are resisting the policy reform necessary to tackle climate change, just as they resisted financial regulation policy. Will the interaction of distorted incentive structures and regulatory capture be as damaging for climate change policy as it was for financial policy? Perhaps, but political communities in all countries are much more deeply engaged with climate change than they were with financial regulation. This creates an opportunity for autonomy for any government that seeks to use it.

In financial policy, the future of democratic capitalism will hinge on the capacity of governments to act independently of vested interests. With climate change, the future of human civilisation is probably at stake.

Threats to the Open Trading System

The Great Recession comes at a time when open trade is already under threat. Columbia University professor

Jagdish Bhagwati recently documented the collapse in commitment to liberal trade associated with the proliferation of preferential trading agreements in the early twenty-first century.[4] The introduction of climate-change mitigation measures has so far been associated with distortions of international trade in goods; and discussion of emissions trading systems in Australia and the United States suggests that the distortions are about to become much larger.

Many elements of the economic recovery packages created in response to the Great Recession favour particular industries differently across countries. For the time being in the financial services, automotive and some other industries, the pattern of public subsidy is an overwhelmingly important determinant of competitiveness in international trade.

The recession has also further reduced the appetite for completion of the Doha Round of multilateral trade negotiations. Subsidies have been reintroduced for agricultural exports from the European Union and the United States.

The weakening of open multilateral trade is bound to damage recovery in the global economy. Broadly based global recovery requires the re-establishment of confidence in open trade, which in turn requires major efforts to correct each of the new impediments to trade. This requires first of all the completion of the Doha Round and also a comprehensive global agreement on climate change mitigation that removes the rationale for assistance to trade-exposed industries.

There was a time during the Cold War when US leadership galvanised commitment to multilateral trade liberalisation among the market economies. Now that moment has passed. It is not clear from whence will come the necessary leadership for reversing the drift into protectionism that has accelerated in the aftermath of the Great Crash.

Financial Regulation and Investment

It is now recognised that in an increasingly integrated world financial system, many aspects of regulation require international cooperation to be effective. But the institutions and instruments of this cooperation remain weak in comparison with the mechanisms for domestic regulation. However desirable international supervision of globally significant financial businesses may be, there is no path to it for the time being.

Nor is there any current path to the international sharing of the costs of failure of supervision. The expense of bailing out failed financial institutions fell on the home governments in this crisis, and there is no appetite for spreading the load. While international consultation can play a role in sharing views on policies and approaches, monetary and financial regulation will remain national for the time being.

The combination of high savings rates and a rapidly growing economy in China relative to the United States raises some difficult issues in relation to the ownership of capital and to the preservation of open markets for direct foreign investment. The accumulation of capital has its origin in saving. The countries that have been growing most rapidly, first of all China, save much higher proportions of their incomes than the old industrial economies. In standard national accounts terms, the Chinese economy in 2008 was a bit above 30 per cent the size of the US economy, while the absolute size of its savings were slightly larger and rising more rapidly.[5]

The relative decline in savings in the old industrial countries did not matter so much to the allocation of capital resources before the Crash. A small number of international financial conglomerates played the main role in taking savings from the surplus to the deficit countries. This involved specialised expertise accumulated over decades and centuries. New York and London have been the leading financial cities, with the others a long way behind in scale and influence.

The collapse of international financial intermediation in September and October 2008 removed a rich source of income from the global financial centres. More importantly, it broke the arrangements that allowed firms to fund the purchase of assets from others' surplus savings, and forced the savers to seek ownership of business assets. It did this at a time of historically low asset prices after the Crash, allowing the savers to quickly build strong equity positions if they had the mind to do so.

Among much else, this is already changing attitudes in the established industrial countries to free movement of capital and in particular to direct foreign investment. The old system of international financial intermediation allowed the surplus countries' savings to be deployed in companies owned anywhere, but especially in the developed countries, for investment in the development of businesses anywhere.

Without the global financial conglomerates playing major roles, new channels of capital flows are required. One is the direct purchase of government bonds in deficit countries—a major source of East Asian capital flows to the United States. Another is the purchase of equity in businesses. The latter has become more important since the Crash, but has prompted visceral political reactions in some developed countries. The reactions are likely to lead to some diversion of capital flows from the countries in which they might have been employed at greater value, to countries in which they are welcome.

There are two end points of the process. One is to compound the factors generating large pressures for the contraction of payments deficits through the large and sudden reduction of incomes and expenditure. The other is to increase restrictions on international direct investment, especially to developed countries. Both will add to the difficulties of sustaining strong growth in the aftermath of the Great Crash.

12

Chaining the Elephant

THE AUSTRALIAN BUREAUCRAT PUSHED his anxious goblin face into the desk in front of him and raised his eyes towards the surrounding television cameras and senators. 'It was certainly my understanding that the original representation ... came from the Prime Minister's Office ... But my memory may be faulty, or completely false,' he said.

Godwin Grech was the Australian Treasury official charged with administering the emergency facility set up to fill the gap in retail car financing after the collapse of US suppliers in the Great Crash. At issue was whether the Prime Minister of Australia had exercised undue influence in favour of a political benefactor who was a dealer in used motor vehicles.

Grech's evidence to the Senate committee was explosive. It seemed to confirm the allegations of the Leader of the Opposition, who had been referring to an email sent from the Prime Minister's Office to the Treasury. He had called for the Prime Minister's resignation.

Grech was right to say that his recollection may have been faulty, or completely false. A Federal Police investigation revealed that the notorious email was a forgery, and that Mr Grech was associated with its creation and dissemination. It was now time for the Prime Minister to call for the resignation of the Leader of the Opposition.

Australia was absorbed by the high drama. The Great Crash and its recessionary aftermath were for a while far from the public mind. But there was almost no reflection on the substantive message from this bizarre incident. Following the Crash, huge amounts of money were being disbursed from the public purse to a wide array of activities and enterprises whose bailing out was seen as important to economic stabilisation and recovery. Officials' decisions rather than competitiveness in the marketplace now determined the fortunes of many businesses.

One lesson from the Great Crash is that more effective regulation of financial markets is required. But this does not mean greater regulation of markets or government intervention in the economy more generally. The early policy response risked entrenching rationalisations for much more widespread state intervention in markets. This would impose persistent high costs on the integrity of our democracy as well as on our market economy. There are equally important lessons for macro-economic policy.

This chapter discusses how to avoid a return of the Great Crash elephant through finding the right balance of economic management, financial regulation and free markets. The final chapter examines the ideological legacy that will underpin this balance. It is at once less certain and potentially more damaging.

The Legacy for Macro-economic Policy

The Great Recession that followed the Great Crash should leave an important legacy of ideas and practice for macro-economic policies. But it may not. In Australia, the senior Treasury and central bank officials responsible for macro-economic policy have taken early opportunities to explain why monetary policy should not be influenced by asset bubbles and external payments imbalances.

However, the early official response is unlikely to be the last word. There was debate during the technology stock market bubble of the 1990s, and again in the early twenty-first century, about whether high and rising asset prices warranted a tightening of monetary policy. At the time, the dominant view was that they did not. Adjustment of policy in response to asset bubbles was seen as inconsistent with 'inflation targeting': the guide to monetary policy in most developed countries. Monetary policies were tightened when expectations of increases in the prices of goods and services rose above an acceptable and known range. The tightening would continue until price rises or expectations of them were back within the range.

The defenders of pure inflation targeting still argue for moving interest rates only when inflation in the general price levels of goods and services is tending outside the preferred range. According to this view, if asset price distortions are a problem, other instruments of policy would be used to correct excessive movements in these markets. It is not clear whether there are any such instruments that could have sufficient impact and not also affect interest rates.

The alternative view is that asset as well as general goods and services prices are relevant to monetary policy. When these prices are moving in very different ways, as was the case in the Platinum Age boom prior to the food price increases of 2007 and 2008, there will be an awkward need for the exercising of judgement. Such an awkward moment would arise if, in the period immediately ahead, asset inflation was strong while goods and services inflation remained weak.

The big test will come in the next asset price boom. It is unlikely that the awful experience of this decade will be ignored.

In macro-economic policy, there will also be a shift in thought about whether large imbalances in external payments are a reason for concern. As we have seen, global imbalances were not the sole cause of the Great Crash. Panics and Manias, Clever Money and Greed all played their part. The Anglosphere asset boom was turbocharged by the availability of cheap credit from abroad. But it could and probably would have advanced a long way on domestic finance alone.

The special contribution of the global imbalances was to increase the vulnerability of real economic activity to financial crisis. This experience will restore awareness of the vulnerability of economies with unusually large external imbalances. We say restore, because there was once widespread and acute awareness of this vulnerability. The experience of many financial crises and recessions came to seem irrelevant in the new world of floating currencies from the 1970s and 1980s.[1]

Nowhere was the complacency about external payments deficits more pronounced than in Australia. Imbalances came to be accepted if they were the result of private expenditure exceeding private incomes. Australians might have taken heed of the Asian Financial Crisis, where shortfalls in private savings in Thailand, Korea and Indonesia in particular led to huge declines in economic activity. But these warnings were ignored.

There is no comfort in a deficit having its origins in excessive private debt. In a crisis, private obligations become public liabilities in an afternoon. The Australian Treasury before the Crash had become a voluble defender of the view that current account imbalances are irrelevant to macro-economic policy. A senior Treasury official responsible for monetary policy in June 2009 listed the payments imbalances as the first cause of the Great Crash and the Great Recession.[2] It would be difficult to reconcile this view of the past with the view that imbalances should not be taken into account in future policy.

Whatever the official view, individuals in their personal and corporate roles will be more cautious in accepting or funding excessive debt while the memory of the Great Crash lasts. This will limit the scale of international imbalances for some time. In East Asia, there will be a new awareness of the risks associated with exceptionally large payments surpluses. The lessons will not be burned as deeply into the brains of the surplus countries; adjustment to new patterns of growth is easier for them. But it will still be influential. East Asian countries will seek to make domestic demand growth more central to their economic strategies.

There will be one other influential message for macro-economic policy. The commodity exporting countries will be strengthened in their understanding of an old wisdom. If expenditure, both government and private, is allowed to expand too much when commodity prices are exceptionally high, there will be dreadful problems when it becomes necessary to adjust to lower living standards as prices fall to more normal levels. As a result, it is prudent to spend only a small part of the gains from commodity price increases until enough time has passed to demonstrate that they are here to stay.

This understanding will end up being most vivid to Australians. They were the spendthrifts of the early Platinum Age commodities boom.

The lessons for fiscal policy in recession will depend on what happens next. The prescription from economic analysis is clear, that major fiscal expansion is warranted in response to deficient demand. The concerted expansion in many countries is easing recession. But its success in promoting recovery may not be remembered as clearly as the public debt that will remain, even though the total public and private indebtedness will be no higher than it would have been without the budget deficits and the associated recovery. And to the extent that the fiscal expansion has been too small to secure recovery, the poor future performance is as likely to be attributed to the failure of expansionary policies as to their inadequate size.

The risks of a return of the Great Crash elephant are high enough for it to matter that we draw the correct conclusions.

The Legacy for Financial Regulation Policy

Banking's raison d'être is to make appropriate judgements about the risks attached to borrowing and lending with real customers. The banker has a difficult, boring, subtle and, above all, local task. The reward is in the profits that flow from correctly judging the risk and therefore the spread between the banker and the borrower. The profits can be immense because those who are thought to do it safely are able virtually to create money.

But if the banks go wrong, it is not only their owners and employees who suffer great loss. With the opportunity for exceptional profit goes responsibility. It is for this reason that for a long time in all countries, banking has been surrounded by special rules that include requirements to hold an adequate amount of capital in reserve.

However, the contemporary global system of finance distorted, disguised, hid and forgot risks that were as real as bricks and mortar. The Great Crash revealed these flaws in the main financial institutions through which capital was allocated throughout the modern global economy. A costly financial crisis was not an unlikely event—if the global financial system were reconstructed in its old image, the Great Crash or something like it would return. The big lessons for policy are about the need for fundamental reforms in the structures and regulation of modern finance.

It will not be easy to remove the flaws that caused the Crash. First of all, the regulatory weaknesses arose from a political economy that has not been fundamentally changed by the crisis. The interests that benefit from the weaknesses in the system continue to invest a substantial part of their profits in the political system to perpetuate the flaws. The central problem that needs to be corrected is the interlocking set of arrangements that encourages short-term, risky investment. Five factors interact to encourage imprudent risk-taking:

1 Standard remuneration arrangements for senior executives are based on profits or share prices over periods that are too short to bring the full consequences of business decisions to account.

2 Standard means of measuring profit in the financial sector bring a large part of expected future prof-its to account when a transaction is made, rather than when the success of the transaction has been demonstrated.

3 Standard models used for measuring and evaluating risk in financial markets systematically underestimate the likelihood of extremely adverse outcomes. In so doing they help to promote those outcomes.

4 The specialist institutions that attribute risk to invest-ments, instruments or enterprises are compromised by receiving high proportions of their incomes from

entities that benefit from favourable (that is, 'low risk') ratings. There is a similar problem of conflict of interest in the provision of advice on executive remuneration.

5 Most difficult of all, it will be necessary to change the attitude that has developed among the largest players in the financial markets, that investment is a one-way bet. The elephant will remain unchained for as long as financial market participants believe that giant bets will make them rich if they succeed, and will be picked up by the ordinary citizen if they fail.

No-one within the financial institutions, their remuneration advisers, the rating agencies or even the regulatory agencies has a personal interest in correcting these fatal flaws.

These distortions in the markets for capital and financial services have been exacerbated by the manifold interventions of government during the crisis. The errors have been covered up with public money. Those responsible for gross errors have been left with the gains from the times before the bets went wrong. The people who were still in their financial sector seats when the markets collapsed are mostly still in them as this book goes to press, expecting to be richly rewarded as the markets lift from the nadir of late 2008. This is moral hazard on a scale the world has never known before.

In the immediate future, behaviour in the markets will be modified by the recent memory of catastrophe. For a while, investors will be reluctant to invest in assets that look risky above the norm. High prices will be required for capital in any venture that, in the superficial ways in which the markets judge these things, looks risky on account of its location or nature or other characteristics.

We will now see more effort going into analysis and the development of regulatory regimes. In the meantime, clearer identification of the problem is needed by people from outside the system. Public analysis of the roles and approaches of remuneration experts, more critical supervision from large shareholders, and public and shareholder commendation of boards of directors that get it right should be encouraged.

What can we say about the qualities of a good regulatory system in light of the Great Crash? It would be better if we were not starting from here! The global economy would face less risk of instability if then Federal Reserve Chairman Paul Volcker had won the battles over regulation back in 1987. It would be better if the economist James Tobin's assertions in defence of Volcker had been more influential: to separate deposit-taking from other institutions; to avoid banks being too big to fail; to apply strict and cautious capital adequacy requirements and regulation of investments by deposit-taking institutions; and to deny regulatory protection to other institutions.[3]

Through these initiatives, global finance could have retained the dynamic capability to intermediate savings for productive investment in commercial activities and infrastructure globally, while holding systemic risk to acceptable levels.

But the reality is that the contemporary acceptance of close integration between traditional and investment banking will survive for now. The window of opportunity for Tobin-type regulatory reform in the Anglosphere has closed, at least until the return of another Great Crash elephant. So what can we say about the preferred qualities of a second-best regulatory system? Four points can provide a start.

First, such a system should discourage the monopolisation of the financial services business, and promote competition. It should seek to avoid the emergence of banks that are too big to fail. Australia's ban, since deregulation, of mergers among major financial institutions provides a positive example. The encouragement of new deposit-taking institutions with conservative approaches to lending would help.

Second, institutions involved in deposit-taking and including investment banks must be subjected to rigorous regulation to remove any significant probability of institutional failure. All regulated financial institutions need to be subject to high capital adequacy provisions. It should be crystal clear that any firm outside this regulatory framework is on its own. A firm's owners, bond holders and creditors should not have the slightest doubt that if a firm fails, they will lose all of their money if the assets of the firm are not large enough to cover them all.

Third, it should retain mark-to-market accounting strictures and close the off-balance-sheet loopholes that enabled banks to surreptitiously increase leverage. The closing of off-balance-sheet activities should include all derivatives. These must be brought onto open exchanges where investors and regulators alike can make judgements about the prospects for a firm, or the systemic risk raised by interconnection.

Fourth, it should treat the provision of credit ratings as a public good. These should be funded by public institutions, national or international. The rating agencies should be regulated through the financial sector arrangements.

Fifth, steps must be taken to reduce the influence of vested interests in the policy process. This is a matter of great complexity and difficulty. As an essential first step, there is a need for strong constraints on movements between business, including lobbying, and related official roles, extending over lengthy periods. More generally, firm steps are required to block the use of financial power to buy political access and influence.

A sixth requirement is the reform of executive remuneration, to remove incentives to take unreasonable risks with other people's money. Regulation can usefully require approval by shareholders and complete disclosure. Beyond regulation, this is a major challenge for directors, for shareholders and their representatives and for civil society more generally. The current inquiry by the Australian Productivity Commission should provide an analytic basis for Australian debate of these issues.

13

Private Interests, Public Good

IN THE CHINESE OASIS town of Dunhuang, way out west on the edge of the Gobi Desert, lies one of humanity's great artistic creations. Over thousands of years, travellers stopped here on their long journey along the Silk Road that connected China to the rest of the ancient civilised world. During their repose, many added to the paintings in the local caves, sometimes working over earlier creations.

We do not know the names of the authors of these great works. And so it is with most of the contributions to the great structures of human civilisation, made by many millions of minds and billions of hands. An act of genius hundreds of thousands of years ago formed the first words, in the first language, followed by the myriad acts of genius that created all of the languages through which humans have spoken to each other. It required genius to build and then enhance the innumerable practices that have bound all human societies, from the most primitive to the most advanced, and enabled people to live together in imperfect harmony. These acts of genius are not attributed to individuals now and rarely generated wealth for their authors at the times of their creation.

Then some creative genius observed that the rate of material progress accelerated if the individuals responsible for leading productive change gained a substantial part of the value that it generated, a notion that took hold initially in Western Europe and then in more and more parts of the world. It has remained true that not all valuable creative acts lend themselves to reward for the person or people held to be responsible for them. In many areas of human endeavour, and probably in most of the areas that have been the most important to the welfare of our species, innovation has only generated small material rewards.

Nevertheless, the abundant rewarding of individuals for leadership in mundane matters related to material progress has left us all better off. Societies have prospered if they have organised themselves to apply this insight. The social benefits have required the acceptance of arbitrary outcomes: some acts of creation and leadership have been rewarded with individual wealth, while others, including the most important, have not.

In the late twentieth and early twenty-first centuries, the idea that individual effort should be rewarded with wealth was pushed beyond the limits upon which the modern market economy had been built. An idea grew in some places that humanity was the sum of its parts, and that an individual alone made her own good or ill fortune. This idea was more influential in the advanced industrial countries, the democracies and especially in the Anglosphere. The idea was absorbed into the rationalisation of the incentive structures that became important in the business world. Chapter 5 discussed how the embracing of this within the financial sector over recent decades was part of the cause of the Great Crash.

This view that an individual could achieve financial or any other goals independently of society always was an illusion. A market economy requires an elaborate set of shared ideas and values to constrain individual behaviour. The illusion was most clearly formed in the countries in which social organisation and institutions were so highly developed that they were taken for granted. People who are deeply conscious of society at an early stage of a market economy are more closely aware of the importance of shared values, institutions that shape human behaviour, and constraints on the personal maximisation of incomes or wealth.

In *The Wealth of Nations*, Adam Smith's views on economic life—the perspectives that began modern economics—were developed from close knowledge of such a society. Smith's earlier book, *The Theory of Moral Sentiments*, explored the many ways in which humans respond to commendation and disapproval, as well as to the needs, happiness and misfortune of others. These moral sentiments are the building blocks that allow humans to live together in modern society. These are the constraints that shape the values of tolerance, honesty and forbearance on which a market economy and a functional polity are built.

No person who has been close to the agony of development in a new market economy—China, or Indonesia, Papua New Guinea, India or any of the countries of Africa—would say that the unconstrained market can cure all ills, or that there is no such thing as society. The same refrain would be absurd to anyone who has lived where there is no established respect for law, or no internal and private constraints on the use of public office to gain personal wealth. No-one with this background would advise a country without any history of a market economy to move quickly to a reliance on market exchange.

It is to their disgrace that some foreign economists advised just this to the successor states to the former Soviet Union in the years immediately after the collapse of rule there by the Communist Party. China's Communist Party was successful in its reform efforts partly because it understood the country's underdevelopment. It took no such leaps, and allowed time for the building of new institutions.

The importance of constraints on private enrichment is greatest in a democracy. Elements of any society can disrupt order and the functioning of public institutions in ways that are damaging to development, but the opportunities for such disruption are more widely available in a democracy. These elements can be expected to use their veto against stability and progress unless each of them feels that the benefits of policy are being fairly shared.

An economist with the International Monetary Fund, Fred Hirsch, introduced a subtle treatment of these issues into modern economic literature in the 1970s. In *Social Limits to Growth*, Hirsch argued that the modern market economy is successful only to the extent that it stands on the shoulders of a pre-capitalist ideology. He was concerned that the growth and maturation of the market economy undermined the moral and ideological foundations upon which it depended. The market economy depends on respect for rules that cannot be enforced by law alone. It depends on the owners of business being permitted to maximise their own wealth and incomes in certain defined ways, and on others in society foregoing the opportunity to take advantage of their own positions to do likewise.

Hirsch presented a pessimistic prognosis for capitalism and the market economy that resonated through the Great Crash of 2008. 'As the foundations weaken', he concluded, 'the structure rises ever higher'.[1]

This is the context in which we should discuss the ideological legacy of the Great Crash.

Libertarianism, Liberalism and Neoliberalism

There is a 'libertarian' rather than a 'liberal' or 'neoliberal' view of society that says that individuals can be left to pursue their own interests independently of social constraints. This view is associated with the writings of Ayn Rand, among others. The major figure in public policy who acknowledged the strong influence of such views was Alan Greenspan.

Greenspan said that he believed that the owners of capital—the shareholders of firms—could be relied upon to avoid taking decisions that placed the firms at risk. This view freed regulators from concern about rules or regulations. They needed only to wind themselves back and the market would allocate available capital in the most productive manner possible.

After the Great Crash, in October 2008, Greenspan repudiated this approach in a mea culpa before Congress. 'Those of us who have looked to the self-interest of lending institutions to protect shareholders' equity, myself included,' he said, 'are in a state of shocked disbelief'.

Greenspan's apostasy is the end for the time being of explicit libertarianism close to the levers of power in major countries. It also needs to be the beginning of a new search for a sustainable, productive balance between constraints on and freedom for private maximising behaviour in a modern market economy. The new balance will include tighter and more effective regulation of the financial sector. It will include rigorous regulation or corrective fiscal measures whenever there are large external costs resulting from decisions by private entities that can be corrected at a lower cost than is imposed by the market imperfection itself.

But it will eschew government intervention in markets where this is not justified by clearly identified failures, and by rigorous analysis of the costs of correcting the market distortions. Otherwise there is a risk that the undisciplined expansion of government interventions will increase the use of government power to support private rather than national interests.

The new balance will recognise the importance of equity and environmental amenity as well as economic efficiency as objectives of policy.

The lightly regulated market economy has always been tolerated rather than embraced in the late twentieth and early twenty-first centuries. Following the Crash, it is now under fundamental challenge everywhere. The tolerance was warmest in the Anglosphere, and there it will be most severely tested by the longstanding fiscal hangover from bailing out finance.

Australian Prime Minister Kevin Rudd wrote in an essay in *The Monthly*:

> The time has come, off the back of the current crisis, to proclaim that the great neo-liberal experiment of the past 30 years has failed, that the emperor has no clothes. Neo-liberalism, and the free-market fundamentalism it has produced, has been revealed as little more than personal greed dressed up as an economic philosophy. And, ironically, it now falls to social democracy to prevent liberal capitalism from cannibalising itself.[2]

Similar sentiments have been articulated by heads of government in the United States, the United Kingdom, France and Germany.

Such attitudes are creating a generalised justification for increased government intervention in the economy. This is an environment that encourages rent-seeking behaviour in the corporate sector and soft responses from government. Too-big-to-fail is now a general catchcry that is used by any large employer that has fallen upon hard times. The possibility of business failure and reductions in employment become arguments for exemptions from all manner of regulation that has been applied in the national and international interest. It becomes the basis for sympathetic consideration of all manner of subsidies to individual businesses. It is an organising point for business leaders' resistance to regulation that doesn't suit their private interests.

Protection is always easier politically than free trade. Its premises and lines of argument appeal to the democratic polity. The natural prejudices of humanity are reinforced by investment in political processes by businesses that gain from preferential treatment.

The Great Crash will leave another long and costly legacy in developed countries if it weakens commitments by governments to open and competitive markets. In these markets, success goes to the firms that use resources most efficiently, in the places in which goods and services can be produced at the lowest cost.

The search for a new balance between individuals maximising their personal gain and the common good is not helped by a distinction between historical positions of mainstream 'liberals', 'conservatives' and 'social democrats' in the developed countries. Prime Minister Rudd's 'past 30' years in Australia encompasses roughly equal periods of social democrat (Labor) and conservative (Liberal–National) administrations. Market-oriented reform has been the exclusive preserve of neither. Indeed, the most far-reaching reforms have been undertaken under Labor administrations, and have been widely and accurately assessed as having contributed to a marked improvement in Australian economic circumstances.

Both Labor and conservative administrations modified income distribution in favour of those on lower incomes through adjustments to the taxation and social security systems. Both placed considerable emphasis on regulating aspects of financial market behaviour. This seems to have limited the problems of the Australian financial system.

In the United States, while the first initiatives of financial deregulation lay with the Republican Reagan administration, they were continued under successive Democrat and Republican presidents. The fateful last step in removing constraints on the investment banking operations of the deposit-taking banks—the repeal of the Glass-Steagall Act—was the work of the Democrat Clinton administration.

The category 'neoliberalism' may help a little bit in identifying what went wrong in the lead-up to the Great Crash. Old-style liberalism, which we can call paleoliberalism, came out of the work of Adam Smith and John Stuart Mill. It recognised the importance of a sound moral and institutional framework for a successful market economy. Within that framework, it made a case for the freedom of market exchange, and required the state to give good reasons for influencing the allocation of resources that emerged from market transactions. The so-called 'neo'liberalism of the late twentieth and early twenty-first centuries represented a reassertion of some of that old wisdom. It was influential in bringing a much larger part of humanity within the beneficent reach of

modern economic growth. It was an element in the rise of
the Platinum Age and in the reduction of human poverty
at a rate that had never before been known.

There was a fault in some but not all of the exposi-
tion of liberal ideas about economic policy in the past
few decades. The mistake was to ignore or underplay
the essential role of law, institutions and moral restraint.
These are vital in constraining market outcomes to secure
socially, environmentally, politically or economically
sustainable development. The moral and institutional
framework was taken for granted. This was most dangerous and costly in relation to the financial sector.

The universe of ideas within modern economics
can handle these issues well enough so long as we are
open to the whole. The whole includes the objectives of
policy alongside economic efficiency, the special issues
that surround the supply of public goods, and income
distribution. But the wider framework often has been
lost as economic ideas have become instruments in the
wars fought by commercial interests over policy, and
have been simplified in popular discourse.

Now we must move beyond the oversimplifications
and the slogans. There is now no alternative to the
careful application of old ideas to the new circumstances
that have been revealed by the Great Crash. It would
be a mistake, one with fateful consequences, to expand
the role of government in the economy in general. To
do this at the same time as hanging back from the
hardest and most necessary interventions in the financial
sector—that would be to throw out the baby and keep
the bathwater.

NOTES

INTRODUCTION

1 Kindleberger, Charles P, and Robert Z Aliber, *Manias, Panics, and Crashes: A History of Financial Crises* (5th edition), John Wiley and Sons Inc., New Jersey, 2005.

2 Akerlof, George A and Robert J Shiller, *Animal Spirits: How Human Psychology Drives the Economy and Why it Matters for Global Capitalism*, Princeton University Press, Princeton and Oxford, 2009; Robert J Shiller, *Irrational Exuberance* (2nd edition), Random House Inc., New York, 2005; and Robert J Shiller, *The Subprime Solution: How Today's Financial Crisis Happened and What to Do About It*, Princeton University Press, Princeton and Oxford, 2008. Ferguson's long history of money covers similar ground to Kindleberger on the topic of booms and panics. In subsequent public comments on the current crisis, he emphasises the risks inherent in exceptional 'leverage'. This refers to the high levels of indebtedness relative to income that characterised the boom of the early twenty-first century. See Niall Ferguson, *The Ascent of Money: A Financial History of the World*, Allen Lane (Penguin Books), London, 2008.

3 A number of English-speaking countries—the United States, the United Kingdom, Australia, New Zealand and Ireland—play special and prominent roles in the developments described in this book. We use the term 'Anglosphere' to describe these countries, mindful that this word has usages beyond this. Thanks to Joe Bianco at Melbourne University for the caution. Spain experienced many of the features of the Anglosphere in its housing boom, bust and recession of the first decade of the twenty-first century. Sometimes we use the term Anglosphere in this book in situations in which it might have been more accurate to have added 'and Spain'. In so doing we avoid the endless repetition of 'the Anglosphere

and Spain' when describing the exceptional boomtime increases in expenditure on housing and consumption. We rely on the reader to remember that sometimes Spain is part of the story.

4 Martin Wolf, a distinguished journalist with the *Financial Times*, has famously emphasised the large imbalances in external payments as a causal factor in the Great Crash. See Martin Wolf, *Fixing Global Finance*, The Johns Hopkins University Press, Baltimore, 2008.

5 Taleb, Nassim Nicholas, *Fooled by Randomness: The Hidden Role of Chance in Life and in the Markets*, Random House Trade Paperbacks, New York, 2005; Nassim Nicholas Taleb, *The Black Swan: The Impact of the Highly Improbable*, Random House, New York, 2007; George Soros, *The New Paradigm for Financial Markets: The Credit Crisis of 2008 and What it Means*, Public Affairs, New York, 2008.

I THE PLATINUM AGE

1 The average growth in this period prior to the Great Crash was as strong as and more broadly based than that of what has come to be known by economic historians as the Golden Age of the 1960s and 1970s. The term was first used in Ross Garnaut's paper in honour of the eightieth birthday of economic historian Angus Maddison, 'Making the International System Work for the Platinum Age'. It is to be published late in 2009 in Thanh Tri Vo (ed), *International Institutions and Economic Development in Asia* (Pacific Trade and Development Series), Routledge Publishing, London 2009.

2 Keene, Donald, *Emperor of Japan: Meiji and His World 1852–1912*, Columbia University Press, New York, 2002.

3 Euromonitor International, from International Monetary Fund, *World Economic Outlook*.

4 Chen, Chunlai, 'Inflow of Direct Foreign Investment', chapter 15 in Ross Garnaut, Ligang Song and Wing Thye Woo (eds), *China's New Place in a World in Crisis*, ANU

E Press, Brookings Institution and (China) Social Sciences Academic Press, Canberra, Washington and Beijing, 2009. Note that dollar values in this book are in US dollars unless otherwise stated.

5 Jha, Raghbendra, *The Indian Economy Sixty Years after Independence*, Palgrave/MacMillian, Hampshire UK and New York, 2008.

6 McLeod, Ross and Ross Garnaut (eds), *East Asia in Crisis: From Being a Miracle to Needing One*, Routledge, London and New York; Arndt, Heinz and Hal Hill, *Southeast Asia in Crisis*, Institute of Southeast Asian Studies, Allen and Unwin and St Martin's Press, 1999.

2 THE GREATEST BUBBLE IN HISTORY

1 'The Danger of a Global House Price Collapse', *Economist*, 16 June 2005.

2 Stock, James and Mark Watson, 'Has the Business Cycle Changed and Why?', NBER Working Papers, 2 August 2002, http://ksghome.harvard.edu/~JStock/pdf/stock&watson_macroannual.pdf

3 Hartcher, Peter, *The Bubble Man: Alan Greenspan and the Missing 7 Trillion Dollars*, W.W. Norton, New York, 2006; Despeigners, Peronet, '"Greenspan Put" May Be Encouraging Complacency', *Financial Times*, 8 December 2000.

4 Wolf, Martin, 'Central Banks Must Target More than Just Inflation', *FT.com*, 5 May 2009, www.ft.com/cms/s/0/34f7848e-39a7-11de-b82d-00144feabdc0.html.

5 Thomas, Hugh, *The Slave Trade: The History of the Atlantic Slave Trade 1440–1870*, Simon and Schuster, New York, 1997, ch 13; Kindleberger, Charles P and Robert Z Aliber, *Manias, Panics and Crashes: A History of Financial Crises*, 5th edn, John Wiley & Sons, Hoboken, NJ, 2005.

6 Cohn, D'Vera, 'Report Details Growth in Illegal Migration', *Washington Post*, 28 September 2005, p. A13, www.washingtonpost.com/wp-dyn/content/article/2005/09/27/AR2005092700735.html

7   US Census, NA-EST2007-01, www.census.gov/popest/
    national/tables/NA-EST2007-01.csv

8   UK National Statistics, 'Population Change', www.statistics.
    gov.uk/cci/nugget.asp?ID=950

9   Australian Bureau of Statistics, Australian Historical
    Population Statistics, 3105.0.65.00, 2008.

10 Shiller, Robert J, *The Subprime Solution: How Today's
    Global Financial Crisis Happened and What to Do about It*,
    Princeton University Press, Princeton, 2008, esp. Chapter 4.

11 In 1995, 667 000 new dwellings were constructed. By
    2000, the number had risen 31.5 per cent to 877 000. In
    2005, dwelling construction was 46.3 per cent higher at 1
    283 000: 'Number of Stories in New One-Family Houses
    Sold', U.S. Census Bureau, www.census.gov/const/C25Ann/
    soldstories.pdf

12 Australian Bureau of Statistics, Australian Social Trends,
    4102.0.

13 Keen, Steve, 'Unmasking the Economics Profession', *Steve
    Keen's Debtwatch*, www.debtdeflation.com/blogs/page/2/

14 Investment Company Institute and Securities Industry
    Association, *Equity Ownership in America 2005*.

15 UK National Statistics, *Share Ownership—Share Register
    Survey Report 2000*.

16 Australian Securities Exchange, *2006 Australian Share
    Ownership Study*, 2007.

17 Standard & Poors/Case Shiller Home Price Index.

18 UK Nationwide House Price Data.

19 Australian Bureau of Statistics, House Price Indexes: Eight
    Capital Cities, 6416.0.

20 US Census Bureau, Current Population Reports, P20-547,
    and earlier reports and unpublished data: from Statistical
    Abstract of the United States, 2008, www.infoplease.com/
    ipa/A0922165.html

21 UK National Statistics, D7252.

22 Australian Bureau of Statistics, Australian Social Trends,
    4102.0.

23 Indicative data from Australian Propert Monitors.

24 'Growth in Buy-to-let Faster than Market as Whole, Says
    CML', *Council of Mortgage Lenders*, 14 February 2007,
    www.cml.org.uk/cml/media/press/1112

25 Reserve Bank of Australia, D02—Lending and Credit
    Aggregates.

26 Holmes, Steven A, 'Fannie Mae Eases Credit to Aid
    Mortgage Lending', *New York Times*, 30 September
    1999.

27 Waggoner, John, 'Sub-prime Woes Could Spill Over into
    Other Sectors', *USA Today*, 19 March 2007.

28 Christie, Les, 'Homes: Big Drop in Speculation', *CNNMoney.
    com*, 30 April 2007, http://money.cnn.com/2007/04/30/
    real_estate/speculators_fleeing_housing_markets/index.
    htm?postversion=2007043011; Harney, Kenneth R,
    'Real Estate Speculation Worries Mortgage Insurers',
    RealtyTimes.com, 21 March 2005, http://realtytimes.com/
    rtpages/20050321_tighterrules.htm; 'Miami's Changing
    Skyline: Boom or Bust?', Justnews.com, 11 March 2005,
    www.justnews.com/news/4277615/detail.html

29 Poulter, Sean, 'Mortgage Madness', *Daily Mail*, 16 October
    2005.

30 Kindleberger, Charles P, and Robert Z Aliber, *Manias,
    Panics, and Crashes: A History of Financial Crises*
    (5th edition), John Wiley and Sons Inc., New Jersey,
    2005.

3 GLOBAL IMBALANCES

1 Wolf, Martin, *Fixing Global Finance*, The Johns Hopkins
   University Press, Baltimore, 2008.

2 Gordon, Max, 'China's exchange rate policy, its current
   account surplus, and the global imbalances', *The Economist
   Journal*, vol 119, issue 541. Also published in Ross Garnaut,
   Ligang Song and Wing Thye Woo (eds), *China's New Place
   in a World in Crisis*, ANU E Press, Brookings Institution

and (China) Social Sciences Academic Press, Canberra,
Washington and Beijing, 2009.

3   International Monetary Fund, *World Economic Outlook*,
April 2009.

4   State Administration of Foreign Exchange, People's Bank
of China. We have followed the convention of measuring
foreign reserves in US dollars, although this does not always
provide a reliable indication of the economic value of the
reserves.

5   Garnaut, Ross, Ligang Song, Stoyan Tenev and Yang Yao,
China's Ownership Transformation, International Finance
Corporation, Washington DC, 2005.

6   Australian Bureau of Statistics, 5206.0, Australian National
Accounts.

4   CLEVER MONEY

1   Galbraith, John Kenneth, *A Short History of Financial
Euphoria*, Penguin, New York, 1994.

2   The term was first coined by Paul McCulley, a bond
manager at PIMCO, and entered the limelight at the Federal
Reserve Jackson Hole meeting in 2007: McCulley, Paul,
'Teton Reflections', PIMCO, August 2007, www.pimco.
com/LeftNav/Featured+Market+Commentary/FF/2007/
GCBF+August-+September+2007.htm

3   *Economist*, 16–22 May 2009.

4   Jones, Sam, 'Commercial Paper Freeze Forced Citi to Double
Subprime CDO Exposure', *FT.com/Alphaville*, 6 November
2007, http://ftalphaville.ft.com/blog/2007/11/06/8630/
commercial-paper-freeze-forced-citi-to-add-25bn-subprime-
cdo-exposure

5   US Federal Reserve Z.1 Flow of Funds Report, 11 June
2009; Annual Flows and Outstandings, 1985–1994.

6   Ibid.

7   Dallas Federal Reserve, *Comptroller's Handbook: Asset
Securitisation*, 1997.

8   Balin, Bryan J, *Basel I, Basel II, and Emerging Markets: a Nontechnical Analysis*, The Johns Hopkins University School of Advanced International Studies (SAIS), Washington, 2008.

9   *Frontline*, 'The Long Demise of Glass-Steagall', Public Broadcasting Service, 8 May 2003, www.pbs.org/wgbh/pages/frontline/shows/wallstreet/weill/demise.html

10 Hempton, John, 'History of US Finance', *Platinum Asset Management*, 4 June 2007, www.platinum.com.au/images/us-finance.pdf

11 Geithner, Timothy F, 'Reducing Systemic Risk in a Dynamic Financial System', remarks at The Economic Club of New York, New York, 9 June 2008, www.newyorkfed.org/newsevents/speeches/2008/tfg080609.html

12 Yeats, Clancy, 'Toxic Assets Leave Black Hole in Highlands Shire's Coffers', *Sydney Morning Herald*, 20 April 2009.

13 Heglund, Corine, 'Why the Financial System Collapsed', *National Journal Magazine*, 11 April 2009.

14 Ibid.

15 Hempton.

16 Ibid.

17 Tett, Gillian and Paul J Davies, 'Out of the Shadows: How Banking's Secret System Broke Down', *Financial Times*, 16 December 2007, http://toodumbtolivearchive.blogspot.com/2007/12/shadow-banking-system.html

18 Securities and Exchange Commission, 'Summary Report of Issues Identified in the Commission Staff's Examinations of Select Credit Rating Agencies', *SEC*, July 2008, www.sec.gov/news/studies/2008/craexamination070808.pdf

19 Moyers, Bill and William K Black, 'CSI Bailout', *Bill Moyers Journal*, PBS, 3 April 2009.

20 Securities and Exchange Commission.

21 *Economist*, 'Triple-A Debt Ratings', 12 July 2007.

22 Dinallo, Eric, 'We Modernized Ourselves into This Ice Age', *Financial Times*, 30 March 2009.

23 Moyers and Black op cit.

24 'Fraudulent ACT Broker Dodges Jail', Mortgage Business, 29 May 2009, www.mortgagebusiness.com.au/breaking-news/2178-fraudulent-act-broker-dodges-jail

25 UBS Report: QBE So far so good Neutral 1227479-4.

26 Australian Bureau of Statistics, Assets and Liabilities of Australian Securitisers, 5232.0.55.001, 2007. These figures are an aggregation of all mortgage assets held by SIVs in Australia, including those that are warehoused, awaiting securitisation.

27 Australian Bureau of Statistics, Assets and Liabilities of Australian Securitisers, 5232.0.55.001, 2007.

28 Reserve Bank of Australia, 'Recent Developments in Collateralised Debt Obligations in Australia', *Reserve Bank Bulletin*, November 2007.

29 Ambac Financial Group Second Lien RMBS Update, 22 May 2008.

30 Australian Bureau of Statistics, Australian National Accounts: Financial Accounts, 5232.0, December 2008.

31 Ibid. APRA calculates the figure at A$381 billion: Reserve Bank of Australia: Bulletin Statistical Table: B12— International Assets and Liabilities of Australian Located Operations of Banks and RFCs.

32 It is not classic shadow banking as we have defined it. The liabilities that the bonds represent are recorded on the bank's balance sheets and are thus subject to capital reserves.

33 Reserve Bank of Australia, Bulletin Statistical Table: B04—Consolidated Group Off-balance Sheet Business.

34 National Australia Bank, 'NAB Half Year Results 2009', Section 6: Supplementary Information, 2009, www.nabgroup.com/vgnmedia/downld/2009HYResultsFinalSec6_HiRes.pdf; AAP, 'NAB May Raise Funds to Cover $4bn in Toxic Debt Losses', 11 July 2009, www.theaustralian.news.com.au/business/story/0,28124,25762361-36418,00.html

35 Australian Bureau of Statistics, Australian National Accounts: Financial Accounts, 5232.0, Table 6: Financial Assets and Liabilities of Banks.

36 De Soto, Hernando, 'Toxic Assets Were Hidden Assets', *Wall Street Journal*, 25 March 2009.

37 Bank of International Settlements, Semiannual OTC Derivatives Statistics at End-December 2008.

38 Bull, Alistair, 'FED FOCUS-Credit Derivatives—a Tool with a Sharp Edge, *Reuters.com*, 16 May 2007, www.reuters.com/article/companyNewsAndPR/idUSN1634150220070516

39 Goodman, Peter S, 'Taking a Hard New Look at a Greenspan Legacy', *New York Times*, 8 October 2008.

40 Sender, Henny, 'CDS Blamed for Role in Bankruptcy Filings', *FT.com*, 17 April 2009, www.ft.com/cms/s/0/5c62b3b2-2adf-11de-8415-00144feabdc0.html?nclick_check=1

41 Das, Satyajit, 'Surreal Realties of the CDS Markets', *RGEMonitor.com*, 16 January 2009, www.rgemonitor.com/financemarkets-monitor/255148/surreal_realities_of_the_cds_markets_-_part_1

42 Bank of International Settlements, *BIS*, www.bis.org/statistics/otcder/dt21.csv

43 Bank of International Settlements, 'Quarterly Review', Table 19, *BIS*, June 2009, www.bis.org/statistics/otcder/dt1920a.pdf

44 Bank of International Settlements, 'Triennial Central Bank Survey—Foreign Exchange and Derivatives Market Activity in 2007', Table B.1, *BIS*, December 2007, www.bis.org/publ/rpfxf07t.pdf

45 Ibid., Table C.1.

46 This assumes that world GDP is $50 trillion.

47 Bank of International Settlements, 'Triennial Central Bank Survey—Foreign Exchange and Derivatives Market Activity in 2007', Table B.3, BIS, December 2007, www.bis.org/publ/rpfxf07t.pdf

48 Ibid., Table C2.

49 Comptroller of the Currency Administrator of National Banks, 'Quarterly Report on Bank Trading and Derivatives Activities Fourth Quarter 2008', Graph 5A, *OCC*, www.occ.treas.gov/ftp/release/2009-34a.pdf

50 Reserve Bank of Australia, 'Survey of the OTC Derivatives Market In Australia', Table 2, *RBA*, May 2009, www.rba.gov.au/PaymentsSystem/StdClearingSettlement/SurOtcDerMarAus/sotcdma_052009.pdf

5 GREED

1 'Bernie Madoff on the Modern Stockmarket', *YouTube*, 13 December 2008, www.youtube.com/watch?v=auSfaavHDXQ&eurl=http://www.advancedtrading.com/regulations/showArticle.jhtml%3FarticleID%3D212500327&feature=player_embedded

2 Szep, Jason, 'U.S. Regulator Probing "Rampant Ponzimonium"', *Reuters.com*, 20 March 2009, www.reuters.com/article/wtUSInvestingNews/idUSTRE52J48B20090320?sp=true

3 Aviram, Amitai, 'Counter-Cyclical Enforcement of Corporate Law', *Illinois Public Law Research Paper No. 07–02*, 28 February 2007.

4 Minsky, Hyman P, 'The Financial Instability Hypothesis', *Working Paper No. 74*, The Jerome Levy Economics Institute of Bard College, May 1992.

5 *Frontline*, 'The Long Demise of Glass-Steagall', *Public Broadcasting Service*, 8 May 2003, www.pbs.org/wgbh/pages/frontline/shows/wallstreet/weill/demise.html

6 Gramlich only privately proposed the investigation into lending fraud, knowing that Greenspan was generally unreceptive to greater regulation: Ip, Greg, 'Did Greenspan Add to Sub-prime Woes?', *Wall St Journal*, 9 June 2007.

7 *Frontline* op cit.

8 Tasini, Jonathon, 'Robert Rubin Gets His Pink Slip', *The Huffington Post*, 10 January 2009, www.huffingtonpost.com/jonathan-tasini/robert-rubin-gets-his-pin_b_156865.html

9 Goodman, Peter S, 'Taking a Hard New Look at a Greenspan Legacy', *New York Times*, 8 October 2008.

10 'Remarks by FDIC Chairman Sheila C Bair to the Global Association of Risk Professionals; New York, NY', *Federal*

Deposit Insurance Corporation, 25 February 2008, www.
fdic.gov/news/news/speeches/archives/2008/chairman/
spfeb2508.html

11   Moyers, Bill and William K Black, 'CSI Bailout', *Bill
Moyers Journal*, PBS, 3 April 2009; Task, Aaron, 'Mortgage
Fraud Epidemic: How the FBI Blew It and Why There's
No "Perp Walks"', interview with William Black, *Yahoo!
Finance*, 6 April 2009, http://finance.yahoo.com/tech-ticker/
article/225823/Mortgage-Fraud-Epidemic-How-the-FBI-
Blew-It-and-Why-There's-No-'Perp-Walks'?tickers=JPM,BA
C,XLF,MHP,MCO,WB,FAS?sec=topStories&pos=9&asset=
TBD&ccode=TBD

12   Taibbi, Matt, 'The Big Takeover', *Rolling Stone*, issue 1075,
March 2009.

13   Kranish, Michael, 'Now-needy FDIC Collected Little in
Premiums', *Boston Globe*, 11 March 2009.

14   Centre for Responsive Politics, *OpenSecrets.org*

15   Jonson, Simon, 'The Quiet Coup', *Atlantic Monthly*,
May 2009.

16   Taibbi.

17   Palmer, Elisabeth, 'AIG Credit Swapper under
Investigation', *CBS News.com*, 19 March 2009,
www.cbsnews.com/stories/2009/03/19/eveningnews/
main4877778.shtml

18   O'Harrow Jr, Robert and Brady Dennis, 'The Beautiful
Machine', *Washington Post,* 29 December 2008.

19   Guerrera, Francesco and Jack Welch, 'A Need to Reconnect',
Financial Times, 12 March 2009.

20   White, Ben, 'What Red Ink? Wall Street Paid Hefty
Bonuses', *New York Times*, 28 January 2009, www.nytimes.
com/2009/01/29/business/29bonus.html

21   Siemaszko, Corky, 'Goldman Sachs Denies Reports It Will
Pay Out Huge Bonuses', *Daily News*, 22 June 2009, www.
nydailynews.com/money/2009/06/22/2009-06-22_financial_
firm_goldman_sachs_to_pay_out_biggest_bonuses_in_
its_140year_history.html

22 Deveney, Christine and Graham O'Neill, *Mercer's Submission to the Productivity Commission Executive Remuneration Inquiry*, 29 May 2009 and company reports.

23 Ibid., and company reports.

24 Ibid.

25 Verrender, Ian, 'Failed Babcock Chalks Up $5.4 Billion Loss', *smh.com.au*, 24 June 2009, http://business.smh.com.au/business/failed-babcock-chalks-up-54b-loss-20090623-cvcs.html

26 Kindleberger, Charles P, and Robert Z Aliber, *Manias, Panics, and Crashes: A History of Financial Crises* (5th edition), John Wiley and Sons Inc., New Jersey, 2005.

27 James, David and Rodney Adler, 'On Freedom and Finance', *BRW Magazine*, 12 March 2009.

6 THINGS FALL APART

1 St Louis Federal Reserve, 'The Financial Crisis Timeline', http://timeline.stlouisfed.org/index.cfm?p=timeline#

2 Rhodes, Elisabeth, 'The Party's Over at Kirkland Mortgage Company', *Seattle Times*, 3 December 2006.

3 The Mortgage Lender Implode-O-Meter, http://ml-implode.com/

4 Onaran, Yalman, 'Lehman Calls Subprime Mortgage Risks "Well Contained"', *Bloomberg.com*, 14 March 2007, www.bloomberg.com/apps/news?pid=20601087&sid=aI6Y2EX7rfj4&refer=home

5 BNP Paribas press release, 9 August 20007, www.bnpparibas.com/en/news/press-releases.asp?Code=LPOI-75W9PV&Key=BNP per cent20Paribas per cent20Investment per cent20Partners per cent20temporaly per cent20suspends per cent20the per cent20calculation per cent20of per cent20the per cent20Net per cent20Asset per cent20Value per cent20of per cent20the per cent20following per cent20funds per cent20: per cent20Parvest per cent20Dynamic per cent20ABS, per cent20BNP

6 'Why Northern Rock Was Doomed to Fail', *Telegraph*, 16 September 2007.

7   Rogers, Ian, 'ABN, NAB and RBS Face RAMS Losses',
    The Sheet.com, 3 October 2007.

8   Boyd, Roddy, 'The Last Days of Bear Stearns', *Fortune
    Magazine*, 31 March 2008.

9   Roubini, Nouriel, 'A Generalized Run on the Shadow
    Financial System', *RGE Monitor.com*, 17 March 2008,
    www.rgemonitor.com/blog/roubini/249924/

10 Setser, Brad, 'It Seems Like So Long Ago ... Documenting
    the Role Foreign Central Banks Played in the US Decision
    to Backstop the Agencies', *Council on Foreign Relations*,
    27 September 2008, http://blogs.cfr.org/setser/2008/09/27/it-
    seems-like-so-long-ago-documenting-the-role-foreign-central-
    banks-played-in-the-us-decision-to-backstop-the-agencies/

11 Mamudi, Sam, 'Lehman Folds with Record $613
    Billion Debt', *MarketWatch*, 15 September 2008, www.
    marketwatch.com/story/lehman-folds-with-record-613-
    billion-debt

12 Williams Walsh, Mary, 'A.I.G. Lists Banks It Paid with U.S.
    Bailout Funds', *New York Times*, 15 March 2009.

13 Dash, Eric and Andrew Ross Sorkin, 'Government
    Seizes WAMU and Sells Some Assets', *New York Times*,
    25 September 2008; Zarroli, Jim, 'Washington Mutual
    Collapse', *All Things Considered*, National Public Radio,
    26 September 2008.

14 Rothaker, Rick, 'Wachovia Sale', *Charlotte Observer*,
    11 October 2008.

15 Australia Securities Exchange, 'Listed Managed Investments
    Monthly Update Feb 2009', ASX, www.asx.com.au/
    products/pdf/lmi/lmi_monthly_update_200902.pdf

16 Nominal Major Currencies Dollar Index, http.federalreserve.
    gov/releases/h10/summary/indexn_m.txt

7   ECONOMIC COLLAPSE

1   Harris, Ethan S, *Ben Bernanke's Fed: the Federal Reserve
    after Greenspan*, Harvard Business School Press, Boston,
    2008.

2   Dow, Christopher, *Major Recessions: Britain and the World, 1920–1995*, Oxford University Press, Oxford, 1998.
3   National Bureau of Economic Research, 'National Economic Trends', 8 May 2009.
4   International Monetary Fund, *World Economic Outlook*, Washington, April 2009, tables A1 and A4.
5   World Steel Association, www.worldsteel.org and various publications.
6   International Monetary Fund, *World Economic Outlook*, Washington, various issues.
7   Ibid.
8   Eichengreen, Barry, 'A Tale of Two Depressions', www.voxeu.org, 4 June 2009.
9   Kindleberger, Charles P, *The World in Depression 1929–39*, University of California Press, Berkeley and Los Angeles, 1973.

8   BAILOUT

1   Stevens, Glenn, 'Interesting Times', address to the Australian Business Economists Annual Dinner, Sydney, 9 December 2008.
2   Gruen, David, 'Reflections on the Global Financial Crisis', address to the Sydney Institute, 16 June 2009.
3   Tobin, chapter 9, traces the 'too big to fail' doctrine for banks back to Continental Illinois in the early 1980s. See James Tobin, *Full Employment and Growth: Further Keynesian Essays on Policy*, Edward Elgar, Cheltenham, UK and Brookfield, US, 2006, p. 91. This is the republication of James Tobin, *Restructuring the Financial System*, Federal Reserve Bank of Kansas City, 1987.
4   Swagel, Phillip, 'The Financial Crisis: an Insiders View', Brookings Papers on Economic Activity, Spring 2009.
5   Hulse, Carl and David M Herszenhorn, 'Congress Rejects Bailout Bill', *New York Times*, 29 September 2008.
6   We had drinks at the United States Embassy in Canberra with the US ambassador and his senior staff on the evening

of 29 September. The ambassador, a confidant of then President George W Bush, explained to us the dilemma facing the lawmakers.

7   'RAW DATA: List of Banks Receiving Funds from $700B TARP', *FOXNews.com*, 5 February 2009, www.foxnews.com/politics/2009/02/05/raw-data-list-banks-receiving-funds-b-tarp/

8   We happened to meet Dr Chalongphob Sussangkarn in Beijing and Dr Sri Mulyani in Melbourne in successive weeks in May 2009.

9   Nocera, Joe, 'Geithner's Plan of Pay Falls Short', *New York Times*, 12 June 2009.

10   Freeland, Chrystia, 'Lunch with the FT: Larry Summers', *FT.com*, 11 July 2009, www.ft.com/cms/s/2/6ac06592-6ce0-11de-af56-00144feabdc0.html

11   Labaton, Stephen, 'Ailing, Banks Still Field Strong Lobby at Capital Hill', New York Times, 4 June 2009; Story, Louise, 'Hedge Funds Step Up Efforts to Avert Tougher Rules', *New York Times*, 22 June 2009.

12   Partnoy, Frank, 'Danger in Wall Street's Shadows', *New York Times*, 14 May 2009.

13   Stevens, Glenn, Governor of the Reserve Bank of Australia, reported at www.theaustraliannews.com.au/business, 30 July 2009.

14   Thornton, Henry, 'We Need Productivity Boosts, Not Sugar Hits', *ON LINE Opinion*, 3 February 2009, www.onlineopinion.com.au/view.asp?article=8496&page=2

15   www.theaustraliannews.com.au/business/story/0,28124,25871774-36418,00.html

16   Reserve Bank of Australia, *Reserve Bank Bulletin*, June 2009.

17   Reserve Bank of Australia, *Reserve Bank Bulletin*, June 2008.

18   Gluyas, Richard, 'Bank Guarantee to Go, Fees under Spotlight', *Australian*, 13 May 2009.

19   See for example James Button and John Garnaut, 'How Henry Kaye fuelled the property boom', *The Age*, 22 September 2003, www.theage.com.au/articles/2003/09/21/1064082867568.html.

20 Stevens, Glenn, address to James Cook University's
    Business Excellence Series in the Tropics (BEST), Townsville
    Luncheon, 4 June 2009.
21 Australian Bureau of Statistics, House Price Indexes, Eight
    Capital Cities, 6416.0, March 2009.
22 Standard & Poors/Case Shiller Home Price Index.
23 'Special Report on International Banking', *Economist*,
    14 May 2009.

9 DEPRESSION ECONOMICS
 1 National Bureau of Statistics (NBS), Beijing. Data from
    Rural Household Survey, 2009.
 2 Keynes, John Maynard, *The General Theory of
    Employment, Interest and Money*, Palgrave Macmillan,
    New York, 2007/1936.
 3 Krugman, Paul, *The Return of Depression Economics*,
    WW Norton & Company, New York, 1999 and 'Depression
    Economics Returns', *New York Times*, 14 November 2008.
 4 Corden, Max, 'The theory of fiscal stimulus: How will
    a debt-financed stimulus affect the future?', Centre
    for Economic Policy Research, Policy Insight No. 32,
    May 2009.
 5 Stevens, Glenn, Governor of the Reserve Bank of Australia,
    reported at www.theaustraliannews.com.au/business,
    30 July 2009.
 6 Naughton, Barry, 'Understanding the Chinese Stimulus
    Package', *China Leadership Monitor*, no. 28, 2009.

10 GROWTH AFTER THE RAMPAGE
 1 Reischauer, Edwin O, *My Life Between Japan and America*,
    Harper and Row, New York, 1986, p. 120.
 2 Garnaut, Ross, 'Is Macroeconomics Dead?', *Oxford Review
    of Economic Policy*, 2005, vol. 21, no. 4, pp. 534–31.
 3 Koo, Richard C., *Balance Sheet Recession: Japan's Struggle
    with Uncharted Economics and its Global Implication*,
    Wiley, Singapore, 2003.

4   The official survey was conducted by the National Bureau
    of Statistics of China. It covered 68 000 rural households
    in 31 provinces. Other official and private surveys give
    broadly similar results. See Sherry Tao Kong, Xin Meng
    and Dandan Zhang, 'Impact of Economic Slowdown on
    Migrant Workers', chapter 12 in Ross Garnaut, Ligang Song
    and Wing Thye Woo (eds), *China's New Place in a World
    in Crisis*, ANU E Press, Brookings Institution and (China)
    Social Sciences Academic Press, Canberra, Washington and
    Beijing, 2009.

5   Chen, Chunlai, 'Inflow of Direct Foreign Investment',
    chapter 15 in Ross Garnaut, Ligang Song and Wing Thye
    Woo (eds), *China's New Place in a World in Crisis*, ANU
    E Press, Brookings Institution and (China) Social Sciences
    Academic Press, Canberra, Washington and Beijing, 2009.

6   Garnaut, Ross, 'Breaking the Australian Complacency of
    the Early Twenty-first Century', 2005 Economic and Social
    Outlook Conference, University of Melbourne, 31 March
    2005, www.RossGarnaut.com.au.

7   Australian Treasury, *Budget Papers, 2009–10*, 2009, www.
    treasury.gov.au

8   Australian Bureau of Statistics, National Accounts, March
    Key Figures, March 2009, www.abs.gov.au/ausstats/abs@.
    nsf/mf/5206.0/

9   Food Policy Research Institute, 'Responding to the Global
    Food Crisis: Three Perspectives', *2007–08 Annual Report
    Essays*, 2008.

11   THE ELEPHANT'S FOOTPRINTS

1   For a general treatment, see Richard Armitage and Joseph
    Nye, *A Smarter More Secure America*, Centre for Strategic
    and International Studies, Washington DC, 2007.

2   International Panel on Climate Change (IPCC), *Climate
    Change 2007*, Cambridge University Press, Cambridge;
    Ross Garnaut, *The Garnaut Climate Change Review,*

www.garnautreview.org.au or Cambridge University Press,
Cambridge and Melbourne, 2008.

3   Estimates from the Netherlands Environmental Assessment
Agency www.pbl.nl/en/publications/2009/Global-CO2-
emissions-annual-increase-halves-in-2008.html

4   Bhagwati, J, *Termites in the Trading System*, Oxford
University Press, New York, 2008.

5   International Monetary Fund, *World Economic Outlook*,
Washington DC, various issues and databases.

12   CHAINING THE ELEPHANT

1   Garnaut, Ross, 'Is Macroeconomics Dead?', *Oxford Review
of Economic Policy*, 2005, vol. 21, no. 4, pp. 524–31.

2   Gruen, David, 'Reflections on the Global Financial
Crisis', Sydney Institute, Sydney, June 2009, www.
thesydneyinstitute.com.au

3   Tobin, James, *Full Employment and Growth: Further
Keynesian Essays on Policy*, Edward Elgar, Cheltenham, UK
and Brookfield, US, 2006, p. 91. This is the republication
of James Tobin, *Restructuring the Financial System*, Federal
Reserve Bank of Kansas City, 1987.

13   PRIVATE INTERESTS, PUBLIC GOOD

1   Fred Hirsch, *Social Limits to Growth*, Harvard University
Press, Cambridge, 1976.

2   Rudd, Kevin, 'The Global Financial Crisis', February 2009,
http://themonthly.com.au/node/1421

INDEX